ABOUT THE AUTHOR

Jegsy Dodd is a lifelong Liverpool fan who has been going to the match solidly for over forty years. He was co-author of 'REDMEN - A Season On The Drink' and 'Here We Go Gathering Cups In May'. He has also been involved in bits and pieces for LFC TV and various fanzines. In the mid-eighties he recorded poetry tracks for the legendary John Peel show on Radio 1, and went on to make a couple of albums with his band 'The Sons of Harry Cross'. After a musical break, he returned with the critically acclaimed album 'Wake Up And Smell The Offy' with his new band 'The Original Sinners'. The poignantly titled 'Only Football Can Truly Break Your Heart' was put out as a single and resonated with the match going public far beyond the city's boundaries. After the album 'Loquacious, Loquacious, Loquacious' he decided to shun the microphone for a life of writing about the adventures and mishaps of following his beloved team.

For more info see www.redmenbooks.co.uk

ON THE ROAD WITH THE
REDMEN

Best Wishes

Jegsy Dodd

JEGSY DODD

Published by Pie and Chips Publishing

Pie and Chips Publishing
401 Portland Court
Wallasey
Merseyside
CH45 2NH

Email: pieandchipspublishing@outlook.com

ISBN 978-0993028-502

British Library Cataloguing in Publication Data.
A catalogue record for this book is available from the British Library.

Typeset in Adobe Garamond Pro by Troubador Publishing Ltd
Printed and bound in the UK by TJ International, Padstow, Cornwall

MIX
Paper from
responsible sources
FSC
www.fsc.org   FSC® C013056

Dedicated to Tommy O'Hagan,
who sadly died on the morning of
the Southampton match,
Saturday 1st March 2014.

A true Red who lived life to the full.
An inspiration to us all.

This one's for you Tom.

Acknowledgements

First of all, thanks to each and every one of you who attended the away games of this unforgettable season. You are the reason why Liverpool FC remains the most unique football club in England. Thank you to the team itself for making this the most entertaining and unforgettable season for years. A massive shout to all the Redmen whose company I have shared on this long and rocky road; Smigger, Ally, Parso, Bucko, Griff, Pooley, Ritchie, Merce, etc, etc. Step forward and take a bow. Special mention to Luke Daly without whose help this book would not have been possible. High fives to Big Keith and Tage for their added assistance and last but not least, the biggest thank you of all to my long suffering partner for her understanding and constant support throughout.

Ally, Smigger, me and Danny in Oslo for the pre-season

Contents

Introduction

It was always going to be a strange experience writing a diary of the season when you don't know what lies in store. Like any year in football, there's always going to be euphoric highs mixed with days of despair and this season was no different. What I've tried to capture here though is to give you an insight into what it's really like travelling around watching the most iconic football club on earth. A sort of fan's eye view of an ever-changing game of drama, theatre, passion and emotion, where every match is a story in itself with kick-off times changed and games moved to satisfy the increasing demand for this new sanitised version of the sport we all love. And this is all against the backdrop of a million sub-plots and weekly debates. This is a book about supporters for supporters. The people who make football what it is today. Like the banner on the famous Spion Kop says 'Football without fans is nothing'.

I decided early on that I wasn't going to cover the home games, for the simple reason that although it's always a joy to go to Anfield, it is also very repetitive. Roughly the same bunch of mates going to more or less the same pubs, and always in the same seat, in the same row of the mighty Kop. Still entertaining, still a good laugh but far more predictable than your average away day. There's always something magical about travelling to watch the boys in red. The whole adventure of being on someone else's patch, in an unfamiliar town; the camaraderie, the solidarity and the complete and utter silliness of the big day out.

We all looked forward to the season with a degree of optimism, now that the club had a more settled feel to it. The protest marches had stopped and those cringe inducing court cases had thankfully also come to an end. There was a better feel about the place in the last year or two that made us supporters think that maybe some sort of challenge could be mounted. The matchday experience is still evolving and people from my generation continue to yawn with resignation as the next batch of political correctness arrives to stifle spontaneity. The ever-growing list of what you are allowed to say and do greets you at the turnstiles. Next season I'll probably have to put my hand up if I want to go to the toilet, or go and get a pie. But then pies will probably have been banned by then anyway. No doubt they would have broken EU law or Health & Safety by having too much pie in them. The Premier League dream is to fill stadiums with the corporate champagne glugging middle classes, and systematically price out the indigenous population. Their vision for the future is probably somewhere like Chelsea where everyone sits in their expensive seats waving little plastic flags in unison as if they were at a royal wedding; everything overseen and choreographed so that no-one has an opinion or does anything spontaneous. Here at Liverpool we frown upon that kind of behaviour.

It's been a season of change not seen in years. Old bacon face has finally left Old Trafford after a lifetime of having the League, the officials and not least the media, firmly eating out of his hand. The man given the job of replacing him was the most successful, unsuccessful manager of all time, a certain Mr David Moyes. Eleven years at Everton and not one single victory at Anfield, and not one single trophy won. A pretty impressive CV I'm sure you'll agree. Over at Man City, the annoying little runt Mancini has disappeared to be

replaced by new man Pellegrini, who seems to be a much more calmer, reserved type of character. Everton have replaced the outgoing Moyes with young Wigan manager, Roberto Martinez. Now you're gonna have to keep this to yourself here, but I actually really like him. This obviously doesn't sit well with me because it is in my DNA to unequivocally dislike any man who is Everton's manager. Secretly I hope he makes some disparaging remark about Liverpool and then normal service can be resumed. And who's that back at Chelski? No, surely not, it can't be. I'm afraid it is. Soft lad is back. The special needs one with the biggest ego in football has returned. No stranger to success or controversy, the brooding little Portuguese pain in the arse will no doubt keep the sports writers happy. So there you have it folks. The scene is set for a season of hopes and dreams. All aways, no homes, no cups and no friendlies. There will be no full match reports, just tales of adventure and tomfoolery in our never-ending pursuit of happiness. That certain happiness you can only get from being a Redman. From the dodgiest pubs to the most hospitable, we've drank in them all. Through the darkest days of defeat to the remarkable ecstatic feeling you get when the boys in red taste victory. No matter how many games you go to, the buzz you get when LFC win never lessens, and long may it continue. This is my personal story of that nine month voyage.

Jegsy Dodd

Saturday 24th August 2013 – 5.30pm kick-off

Aston Villa 0 Liverpool 1

The first away game of the season is always one filled with optimism and excitement. And this is no different, especially after getting off to a winning start against the spoilers from Stoke last week. Everyone is bright eyed and bushy tailed at the prospect of visiting Villa Park, which in recent years has been a happy hunting ground for the mighty Redmen. Today me and Ally have decided to go by train, instead of the coach, for the simple reason that we are the masters of our own destiny. In order words we can go for a bevvy where we want and when we want. And today we want to sample the delights of Birmingham city centre. Brum has always been an uninspiring dour type of place for a country's second city. Never as edgy, arty and exciting as other less populated cities, like Liverpool, Manchester, Bristol, Leeds or Newcastle. But like everywhere, it's had its lick of paint and a bit of a makeover and it actually looks a bit of alright in the August sunshine.

We got off at New Street after a quiet, non-eventful journey down. Hardly any faces on the train except for about thirty boisterous Urchins who got off the back carriage and were soon wrapped up by the police. Stopped, searched, filmed and processed within minutes. We would probably call them spoil sports. They would probably call it preventative policing. But whatever you call it, it has the desired effect and the young Reds are split up into smaller groups and told to leave the station quietly. They skulk away tails between their legs, muttering under their breath. Their bonfire has been pissed on and their balloon has been pricked, but don't worry folks, their songs of victory will be heard again in this city long before Jasper Carrott has had time to put his pyjamas on.

We amble out of the station and into the Midlands sunshine and almost immediately find a boozer tucked up a side road called The Windsor. It's full of Villa fans and about half a dozen Scousers keeping a low profile. We'd only just been saying on the train on the way down here that nearly all city centres look the same nowadays because all the shops are identical multinationals, and that all footy fans more or less look the same. We find a small table hidden out of the way and Ally comes back from the toilet grinning, like he knows something I don't. "What's tickled you?" I say. "You're not gonna believe this. I'm in the bog and a couple of old Villa bruisers say to me 'Alright Scouse, did you come down by train?' and I'm like 'How d'you know we were Liverpool? And they say 'We were onto you as soon as you and your mate walked in'". Ally's asked them how, and they say it's just the way we stroll around the bar area, eyes darting left and right and how we were casually looking over our shoulders when we were waiting to get served. Then the crowning moment, when we sat in the corner with our backs against the wall, where we could subconsciously see the whole pub and more importantly, the door. It's almost like an SAS training manual which has been ingrained into our psyche after years and years of drinking in dodgy pubs at football matches behind enemy lines.

Although we are just a couple of innocent ageing blokes having a quiet bevvy before an away match, there are still certain rules that need to be adhered to. (a) Never sit in the middle of a pub, (b) always sit facing the door so you can see who's coming and going – if you dare to sit with your back to the door you can expect the unexpected, (c) I'm probably warming to the task of explaining this to you now but always have your back to the wall. Now you're probably thinking, 'what's he going on about? He's been watching too many films. Thinks he's some sort of security expert etc.' But my case in point is this. Zenit St Petersburg away earlier this year.

It sounds quite an exotic old place Leningrad, full of mystery and beauty, but in reality it was a cold, grim, uninviting twat of a place, where manners, smiles and politeness were in short supply. We had set up camp for an hour or so in a basement bar on the Nevsky Prospekt when I had clocked a few comings and goings by the door. The bar was half full of foreign Reds who we had little in common with except that we supported the same team. I had mentioned to Ally and Tommy that I was getting a little bit concerned. First three would come in, have a quick butchers, then leave. Then another five would try and slip in unnoticed, then leave without buying a drink. You didn't need to be a fully paid up member of MI5 to suss that the pub was under surveillance by Russian hoolies and it was all about to go a bit half rice, half chips. We necked our bevvies and peeped around the door like Shaggy and Scooby Doo would do in a situation like this, and smartly walked up the steps and outside into the cold St Petersburg air. Next minute about 20 or so agitated Russian baddies are heading towards us. They walk straight past us and into the bar. I've no idea what ensued but there's a good chance they weren't there to hand out tourist information leaflets. The bottom line is whether it's Birmingham or Russia, the same rules apply. You don't go for a gargle in an opposition drinking establishment without a full picture of what's going on. For future reference always remember back against the wall, door in full view. Got it. Good.

Anyway where was I? Oh yeah The Windsor in sunny Brum. Ritchie Tierney walks in off the Euston train and joins us. We have a quick one around the corner in The Shakespeare, say hello to Steve Hitchmough and his mate Paul, and it's a short hop by train to Villa Park. The travelling Reds are in full voice as they pile out of The Witton Arms and up the street to the ground. The first 20 minutes or so is a masterclass of passing and moving by the boys from the Mersey, capped by a fantastic goal by Daniel Sturridge. It's the type of finish Dennis Bergkamp used to do for Arsenal when they were at their peak. Our end is going absolutely crazy, so it's difficult to see if Danny boy is treating us to that god awful disco dancing thing that he usually does when he bangs one in. Yes, I know what you're thinking, it doesn't matter how he celebrates, as long as he scores. And you're probably right but you've got to admit, it's a bit crap. Give me a nutty Robbie Fowler goal celebration any day of the week. We reach the break still 1-0 in front. It's good to see all the old faces, from seasons gone by, full of eternal optimism. That's the thing about supporters, we keep on coming back for more and each and every one of us will be making predictions. You want mine, I would say fourth, but fifth or sixth is probably more realistic. A lot depends on Suarez when he comes back after missing the first six games. I don't think he'll be moody and not give his all. I think he'll just say "ok, let's put it all behind us and I'll give you everything for every match until the end". I don't think he's made any other way. I'm guessing here but if everything went a bit pear shaped for Daniel Sturridge, I could easily imagine him spitting his dummy out and downing tools. Maybe I'm completely wrong. Who knows? We'll see at the end of the season. Don't worry, I won't change what I've written here to make me sound like some insightful visionary when it's all over. No, you'll be getting 19 away games as they happen. There will be no airbrushing or bullshit. If it's great I'll tell you. If it's bloody awful, you'll also be getting to hear about it.

We have a hamburger then as we go back up the steps into the seats there's police cameramen either side of the entrance filming everyone as they pass. It's proper in your face stuff, not discreet at all. I don't know what footage these people are hoping for filming two fifty-something gentlemen coming back from their half-time piss. One off the album perhaps? Or maybe a little song and dance routine for You Tube? Obviously they're not looking for some eloquent half-time punditry from us. What it basically is, is intimidation. Football stadiums are awash with security cameras. The unsuspecting fan can barely pick his nose these days, without the fear of it being shown later on Match of the Day. So I don't think there is any rhyme or reason for the local constabulary to stand a few feet away from your face filming like children with a new plaything. It's not clever and it needs to go. Hang on, West Midlands Police? Weren't they the ones who were supposed to be investigating South Yorkshire Police over the Hillsborough cover-up a few years ago, and found no wrongdoing? It should be us filming them.

Anyway, back to the match. After a scintillating first half, we go onto the back foot and start hanging on in there. It's a bit like the Stoke game last week which we dominated and then took our foot off the gas. Mignolet makes a couple of decent saves and our old friend Benteke goes close, but we have a problem, me and Ally need to get the train from Witton station to New Street at the same time as the final whistle, which means we're gonna have to leg it before the end, which is against all our principles. We bite the bullet and jog down the road coughing and spluttering. Outside the slope to the station there's a bloke in a high-vis jacket beckoning us on. We make it by the skin of our teeth. If we'd have missed it, it would've probably taken us hours to get back via Kuala Lumpur or somewhere. My heart's nearly coming through my chest as some cheeky young whipper snapper offers me his seat. God I must look fucked. It's a turning point in my life. No-one has ever stood up for me before, and although I'm visibly knackered, I now must be officially classed as old. It's a watershed for me as I've always seen myself as a bit of a lad. This is confirmation that what I see in the mirror every day is not entirely the same view as what other people see. Basically the scrap heap is beckoning but I ain't going nowhere without a fight. The train is packed and a roar goes up as the final whistle goes and the Reds manage to hold onto their precious 1-0 advantage. It looks like everyone has had the same idea as us. We've got about six or seven minutes to get some ale before the Liverpool train leaves, which we do without any fuss. The pressure is off and we're homeward bound with the three points and everyone seems happy. It hasn't been one of those crazy days packed with incident but then it's only the first awayday. We've had very little pre-season training so we're bound to be slightly rusty. There was the five night bender in Oslo when we played Valerenga in a friendly in August. And yes that was a bit manic but we're still nowhere near full match fitness. Only regular beer, late nights and sleep deprivation will get us back into full swing for the marathon season ahead.

We get off at Lime Street and dive into Ally's pub on London Road but I'm struggling. After only a couple of swift ones, I'm heading home to the sanctuary of my own bed. I know it is seen as socially unacceptable to be going home before the early hours, but I am genuinely weighed in. There will have to be a vast improvement in my staying power before I embark on the next rigorous test which is an overnight stop in Swansea. I'll have to put in a call to my personal trainer Danny Giles to see if he fancies a few cheeky nights out in the run-up to that one. You know what they say, 'fail to prepare, prepare to fail'. I hope the players appreciate all this hard work we put in behind the scenes.

Monday 16th September 2013 – 8pm kick-off

Swansea 2 Liverpool 2

It's 11am and we're on the road on this epic journey through the Welsh border roads for our 8pm kick off down in Swansea. Ally, who lives in Anfield in the shadow of our place of worship, has picked up a hire car and calls at our house already accompanied by Kirkby's finest one Garry (Smigger) Lundstrom. Parso, who lives in the town with a frown, which is comically known as Birkenvegas, is already at mine and we're ready for the off. I volunteer to drive on the outward journey knowing full well that this morning is the best mental and physical state that I'll be in for the following two days. In other words it's a case of just get your bit out of the way and then you can pass the buck for the predictable nightmare journey home. It probably takes a bit longer going on the A roads instead of the motorway but at least we can stop when and where we want. We plough on past Wrexham, Oswestry, Welshpool and then the roads get really, really windy; bend after bend, unpronounceable village, after unpronounceable village. AND ALL THE ROADS THAT LEAD US THERE ARE WINDING. THERE ARE MANY THINGS THAT I WOULD LIKE TO SAY TO YOU LIKE "WHY THE FUCK DIDN'T WE GO ON THE MOTORWAY?"

After what seems like a lifetime, we stop for food and to empty our bowels in a town without vowels. By the time we get to Swansea and have circumnavigated the city centre's one-way system about twenty friggin' times, I'm emotionally drained. I'm effin' and blindin' at poor old Parso because the battery on his super-dooper sat nav-tastic phone died just when we needed it. What was it he said when we left my house? "You don't need to bring your sat nav, I've got it on me phone" and I'm like "Yeah, but I always take it when I'm on an expedition to a far off foreign land". He looks at me like I'm from an age that time forgot. He waves his phone at me and says "It's all in here, everything you need to know about life is inside this phone". YEAH, everything except fuckin' power. "So Mr Tech-head, Mr Co-driver extraordinaire. Where's the fuckin' hotel?" Parso is lost for words and I'm ranting and raving. My brain's fried and I just want to have a pint and calm down. The other two are making it worse by laughing and going into Morecombe & Wise comedy routines in the back. Now I know full well that pre-sat nav and all that, we always used to just drive somewhere and find it but I'm just letting off a bit of steam.

Six hours jockeying and I've had enough. Ally says "OK, calm down and let's just ask someone". We stop at about six various places and ask about six various locals and they do what everyone does when they ask directions, they just stare at the person's haircut and don't take any information in. "So what did he say Smig?" "Er, dunno, it's down there somewhere" or "I think it's back that way somewhere". Fuckin' marvellous. In the end we pull alongside a Battle Taxi (Police van) and they point us to our accommodation, the Premier Inn. We check in and all the negative thoughts and stress evaporate within seconds. I apologise to Parso, put my bag on the bed and think to myself 'Do you know what, I could get into that bed right now, and do a full eight hours but no, there's people to meet, places to see and pints to be quaffed'. Oh, and I forgot, there's the match as well.

We march out of the hotel and right into the vortex of Swansea.
We are based smack bang in the middle of where it all happens. The
equivalent of a hotel on Mathew Street. Happy days. Happy fuckin'
days. It is no surprise to anyone that the first voice we hear on entering
Lloyds Bar is that of Liverpool's loudest man; the Right Dishonourable
David (Bucko) Buckley AKA Hush Hoskins due to his very slight
resemblance to the actor Bob Hoskins. To the untrained eye you
would think that Bucko was the licensee of this Swansea
establishment. He holds court in the centre of the pub, greeting his
public with warm handshakes and pats on the back. People like us are
even deemed worthy of a mafia style hug each. He beckons people
over to meet other people, even if they don't need an introduction
they are going to get one. He is the ringmaster, the life and soul. He
is the glue that bonds the firm. You could just picture David
Attenborough doing a documentary on him, with that quiet
trustworthy delivery. "Here we see the Alpha Male in his natural
habitat, drinking at the watering hole, surrounded by his troop. When
the sun sets and nightfall descends you will hear his unmistakeable
call. Oh yes, people of south Wales, you WILL hear his call".

We sneak off to the excitingly named 'Railway Men's Club and
Institute' at 42 Wind Street. Some bars have names which conjure up
mental images to entice the paying customer to enter. 'The Secret
Garden', 'Pandora's Box', 'The Cool Room' but with the Railway
Men's Club it is just what you need for a quick half hour's pow wow.
Yes, it looks like a fifties retro formica illegal drinking den, but that's
what we're after. We don't want to be dealing with bouncers, neon,
chrome, and surly sour-faced barmaids. Well, not yet anyway. We'll
deal with all that carry-on after the game. The only late bars open will
probably be the ones that replace the letter 's' with the letter 'z' because

misspelling your product appeals to the spotty gel-headed halfwits who pollute the nation's city centres with their low slung jeans, showing off their undercrackers and making them walk like there's been some sort of cloth-touching incident or an imaginary disability. What is it with these whoppers? They can't put their trousers on properly, they wear their hat the wrong way round, they can't fasten their laces for fear of looking normal and even if they put their stupid fuckin' hood up, it's only half way across their head. I think I've sussed it out. You get ready to go out by only partially putting your clothes on. Nothing's as it should be. Right, next week, I'm getting down with the kids. I'm gonna appear in the pub before the game with me shoes on the wrong feet (how cool is that), one arm in me jacket and the other trailing behind me. Or maybe both arms in me jumper but with me head still inside, peeping out of the neck bit. And just to round it all off, I'll have both socks dangling out of the front pocket of me jeans. Now tell me that's not a good look. Ok, maybe I'll bin the socks.

Anyway fashionistas, we've got to get to the ground and our lovely Premier Inn hosts have laid on a minibus to get us up there. We're supposed to be meeting Ian Mac, Ritchie and Merce at Tom & Jerry's or Ben & Jerry's or Frankie & Benny's by the stadium. It's absolutely rammed but we find them and you'll never guess who's with them, none other than Tommy Trouble. Tommy used to hold the undisputed title of World's Angriest Man. He's mellowed with age now but can still conjure up an exceptional argument out of nothing. It's almost an art form. Back in the day I imagine Tommy would wake up and brush his teeth, have a shave, then suddenly stop and look at his reflection and say "who are you fuckin' looking at?". Oh he's probably offered himself out a few times but it's great to see the fiery old nut job at Swansea away on a Monday night.

We get into the ground and within minutes Jonjo Shelvey scores for them, right in front of us. Jonjo Shelvey of all people. When he played for us he couldn't hit a cow's arse with a shovel. Nice bloke and all that. In fact, not a bad player. But in truth we needed something a little bit better. I always think the sending off at Man United was a turning point when he had a rant at old whisky face as he left the pitch. In all honesty, I don't think he ever recovered from that. He always used to remind me of that bloke in Right Said Fred who were a bit of a novelty act in the eighties and had a hit with the wonderfully titled 'I'm too sexy for my shirt', which funnily enough is exactly what I'm feeling right now, as I write this.

We don't have to wait long before we pull back level with yet another goal from Daniel Sturridge. That's all four games he's scored in this season, which is just what we needed with Suarez being out. I think he likes the responsibility of being the main striker. I don't know how Brendan will accommodate them both when Mr Naughty comes back, but I'm sure he will sort something out. Victor Moses, who we've got on loan from Chelsea, scores on his debut to make it 2-1 to us with about ten minutes to go to the break. I never really rated Moses before he came here, but if he can chip in with a few like that every so often, he'll earn his wages. Again he picked up a stray pass from our mate Jonjo Shelvey and then not to be outdone, Shelvey also sets up their equaliser mid-way through the second half for Mutu, and that's how it finished. A few nervy moments near the end but Mignolet held firm and made a couple of great saves. It's gonna be a night Jonjo Shelvey will never forget, and it is his name that will dominate tomorrow's papers.

We come out of the ground quite thankful to get a point and start walking towards the town centre. After about five minutes our eyes are drawn to another enticingly named pub. Who in their right mind could walk past and refuse a pint in somewhere called The Smith Arms. Certainly not us, that's for sure. I feel better after speaking to a few of the Swansea fans in there, who all think a draw was a fair result. They reckon they could have had a player sent off and been 3-1 down in the first half, which is true. So for them to survive, then put us under pressure in the second half, and get the equaliser, it's seen as a good result. Everyone's happy then. We move on up the road to a place called The Villiers Arms which was alright but no great shakes. The barman phones a taxi for us and weirdly it's the same driver who drove us to the ground in the minibus, yet now he's in a car. He'll probably serve us breakfast in the morning as well. It's only when we get back to Wind Street that it really starts to hot up. There's a load of our away following staying overnight, so the bars along this strip get more and more boisterous as the hours pass by. The local Swansea natives take this small scale Liverpool takeover in good heart. But then again, it is only a Monday night. If it was a Saturday it may well have been a different story with an extra 5,000 pissheads in the area. We spend the last two hours in Popworld which is probably the same as all the other Popworld's around the country, but tonight is different, as tonight it is now Kopworld.

The poor DJ fought a constant battle to try and drown out the inebriated Red crooners. He's trying to mix his tracks and throw in what he thinks are a few crowd pleasers. But half the dancefloor thinks they've entered the 'choir of the year' competition. It's basically a stalemate. The compromise is, if the Redmen like one of his tunes there'll be a mass boogie, with some suspect arm- leg coordination. If they don't give it the thumbs up, it's back to the raucous foot stomping songs of the Anfield Road. I'll tell you what though pop-pickers, the boy Parso can certainly move for a big fella. When he's got his groove on, there's no stopping him. You'd think he was on castors the way he glided across the floor shaking his tail feathers. I, on the other hand, probably look like I was being electrocuted in slow motion. But hey what a night! The first big blow-out of the season and the city of Swansea passes the litmus test with flying colours.

The following morning is in sharp contrast to the previous night, as 'the four lads who shook the world' awake to face the reality of the mother of all hangovers. Breakfast is served and swerved. Fresh orange juice and coffee, yes. Slippery fried eggs, not on your nelly. Strictly Come Dancing hopeful Parso takes the reigns and volunteers to drive. We all realise that to get this car and us occupants home safely is probably going to be on a par with crossing the polar ice caps with a dozen Yorkshire terriers pulling your sledge. It's gonna be a mission but it's just gonna have to be done. Parso, we have faith in you son. Now let's just fire this baby up, burn some rubber and get this road trip under way. He's not messing around either. We're flying around corners and speeding into bends like crazy. Me and Ally are sliding across the back seat like a pair of rag dolls, just desperate for it all to end, but it goes on and on and on. Hill after hill, bend after bend, and we're still in mid-Wales. We stop at a pull-in point halfway up what is probably a really scenic viewpoint but it is wasted on this quartet of good time victims. It's supposed to be a stretch your legs, have a piss and smoke if you smoke stop, but it turns into a honk fest. Ally says "I feel ill. I'm gonna have to throw up". All four of us are lined up facing away from the road, when Ally lets out a grunt and spews about six foot in front of him. Think Mr Creosote in 'The Meaning Of Life', the Monty Python film. Within seconds I'm gagging like a cat with a hairball, and retching. You've got to imagine we're all mid piss at this moment. Parso turns away saying he feels ill as well. Only Smigger seems OK and legs it back to the car to get his phone to try and take a photo. It's a stupid moment. I've got a bubble coming out of my nose because I'm laughing, honking and pissing all at the same time. We calm down and get to the next town where we can get a coffee and maybe try and eat something. I can't remember the name of the place. It was one of those ones that look like you've been given shit letters when you play Scrabble. Somehow we finally get home and Ally, to add to his woes, has to take the car back to the hire place. I don't envy him at all. Even worse he's got to work in the pub tonight. Me, I'm gonna have a nice Radox bath and early night. The team need to work on a few things and we still haven't got the balance right between having a great night out and a bad following day. Early season teething problems need to be sorted out, for both of us.

Sunday 29th September 2013 – 4pm kick-off

Sunderland 1 Liverpool 3

There was a pleasant surprise during the week whilst rummaging through a rarely used drawer in the bedroom. I came across an old friend of mine, my lucky undies. How they had managed to find their way here and not in the appropriate sock or undies drawer is beyond me. Perhaps they felt so ashamed and powerless under the Roy Hodgson regime, that they had fled a couple of drawers down in embarrassment. Unseen for a few seasons I held those ruby red boxer shorts up to my cheek and remembered the good times. I suppose after dropping points at Swansea, getting beat by Southampton, and knocked out of the worthless cup by you-know-who, it's probably fate that has brought us together again. They looked in quite good nick, but then again, I only wore them for the really big games. Maybe they could work that old magic again. Like on those crazy Champions League nights when the stadium rocked under the floodlights as the envious eyes of other Premiership heavyweights paid grudging respect. "What if they're not match fit" I thought. "What if they think it's only Sunderland away and I'm not really arsed". The best thing I could do was to give them a midweek pre-match run-out and see if they are up to the job. My first reaction on wearing them was "Fuckin' 'ell, I don't remember them being this tight!". Had I really expanded this much in just a couple of years? Apparently so. My stomach hung over the waist band like that of a middle aged man that I always promised that I'd never be. And there was the suspicion that on a long coach journey to the North East, that they may well hitch up and leave my Davina's feeling slightly uncomfortable. Mmm, food for thought. I gave them a 24 hour test drive, driving, walking and all the usual activities of modern life, and I am pleased to report that they passed with flying colours. Into the washing basket and they'll be fit for a king come Sunday morning. Who needs a new away kit when you've got bills of this quality and experience? Has an Evertonian's undies ever seen its team tonk Real Madrid 4-0? I don't think so. Has a pair of bluenose bills ever ventured into the San Siro or Nou Camp, let alone gone there and seen its wearer's team leave as victors? Not a hope in hell. Me and these babies are going to Sunderland on Sunday, and we're going to have the time of our lives, and work a little bit of that old red magic.

It's 9am and I meet Dave Johno at the Happy Al's depot in Cleveland Street in Birkenvegas. There's a couple of pick-ups in the Pool of Life. The two major ones are the garage on Scotty Road and the Rocket just as you hit the M62. I've saved Smigger a seat as he must be knackered after travelling all the way from Kirkby this morning. There's always banter because I live in Wallasey and he lives in Kirkby. He reckons the whole of Wirral is part of Wales, so I wind him up about Kirkby being in Lancashire or a suburb of Wigan. After a night in town, the poor lad always has to leave early to get home before sunrise. Whereas I just have to do a hop, skip and a jump and I'm home in twenty minutes. I've always found it weird that people from the Liverpool side of the river always dismiss people from the Wirral side as all being from Birkenhead. It's as if in their eyes Wallasey doesn't exist. And yet Wallasey's population is bigger than that of say Burnley who've supported a Premier league football team. Nearly 100,000. Yet for some strange reason we always get labelled as Birkenhead. Those of you who know a bit about local Wirral history will know that we used to have 2 different councils and 2 town halls, even different coloured buses for fucks sake. The reality is that Birkenhead people don't go to Wallasey and Wallasey people don't set foot in Birkenhead. There's four bridges that separate the two and that remains the front line.

So it's still a mystery how we have collectively become known as Birkenheaders to the Scouse match-going public. I'm sure half of my mates from the game think everyone 'over the water' lives in the same town or village and goes to the same pub. My mate Doggo, who used to have the Weighing Machine pub on Wavertree Road, always used to be looking for pubs on the Wirral and he'd phone up and say "Alright Jegsy lad, I'm coming over by yours later to look at this pub in Eastham. What's it like and who goes in there?" I'm like "How the fuck do I know? It's about 15 miles away. I've never been there and don't know anyone who drinks there". I've been out on the ale more times in India than I have down that neck of the woods. It's like me saying to him "Who goes in that boozer in Widnes or Formby or something. Right I'm gonna move on now because I can almost feel you saying "Shut up you Birkenhead div. Get on with the Sunderland trip".

Right, we're on our way and the sun is shining and the beers are flowing. It's usually at this moment that the cynical side of me creeps in thinking what could possibly go wrong, but today I'm feeling positive. I know Sunderland have just got rid of their predictably unpredictable loonbong of a manager and are bottom of the table, but I still fancy us to get the three points. The Mackems having Di Canio as their boss was the equivalent of our mate Sconch managing

Liverpool. He'd go down at half time if we were losing and batter all the players. If we still didn't turn it around in the 2nd half there would be body bags carried out of the player's lounge after the game.

Anyway we've arrived in the small town of Seaburn about 10 miles from the ground and the venue, which is our host for the next two and a half hours, is the Seaburn Working Mens club. These types of venues are sorted out before we set off, so we don't just arrive and startle the locals. It works both ways. We get a place to have a few sherberts for a couple of hours before the game without confrontation, and they get us to support their social club and help fend off closure for another day. Let's be honest, a coachload of thirsty Scousers can put a lot of money over a bar, so everybody's happy. But first we dive over the road into a pub called The Lambton Arms and then onto The Crosskeys, before we make our entrance. There's only a handful of us, me, Smigger, Ritchie, Mercer, Michael and Jay, so we're easily accommodated. The reason we do this is because if over 50 blokes turn up in one venue at once it is obvious that we could be waiting 15 minutes to get served, and that in anybody's book is simply unacceptable. Eventually we grace the club with our presence and admire the banners from days gone by which adorn the walls. It's a kind of snapshot into the past where you can almost hear the brass bands play as the colliery workers marched behind their union banners in the never ending fight for better working conditions and pay. Slogans such as 'Organisation, the key to economic freedom' are emblazoned across these works of art. Aargh socialism eh! Whatever happened to that? Communities of the working class, unhindered by the drug dealers and wannabe gangsters of today, all pulling in the same direction for the common good. Right, time to take these rose tinted glasses off and head to the game.

I'm standing in the queue when some 'where's Wally' look-alike (all red and white stripes and glasses) starts shouting "Who are yer? Who are yer?" at me. I'm looking around thinking 'does he mean me personally or does he mean LFC'? It's obviously the latter. With that I'm over to him, about a foot away shouting "Who are we? Who are we? I'll tell you who we are, you cheeky little runt! We are Liverpool, the greatest team in English football history, that's who we are". I launch into a tirade of incoherent facts and figures and for some unknown reason I tell him he's that skinny that even 'Purple Aki' would refuse a free squeeze on his non-existent muscles. He just stares open mouthed with absolutely no idea what I'm on about and then the first police officer puts his hand on my shoulder laughing. He's clearly enjoying my comedy outburst and just suggests I calm down and go into the ground and take my seat. The second copper hasn't seen the funny side. "One more word and you're nicked" he says. "Yeah but I was only telling Mr Puniverse a few facts of life, a bit of education for the young lad." He's not impressed and repeats his threat. I decide to keep schtum till we're in the ground but maybe I do seriously need to calm down. I think it's getting worse as I get older. I take the bait every time and then start shouting like a knobhead at everyone. Therapy maybe? No. The counsellor would probably be an Evertonian and I'd end up putting him right on a few things as well. No, I think I'll stay as I am for now.

They've moved our away end slightly so that we're up in the gods like at their rivals Newcastle. I always prefer it when the away support is visible on Match of the Day. You always want to see who took how many to their respective match and how mad they celebrate when they score but not today folks. We're hidden away out of sight but don't worry, you'll hear us. The game is quite open. Martin Skrtel has a goal ruled offside after 10 minutes after a great save from Stevie Gerrard's free kick. Suarez, playing his first league game back since his 10 match ban, is everywhere. If you were a defender he's the type of forward you would hate to play against. Larsson hits the bar for them with a curling free kick before Sturridge opens the scoring for us with as crap a header as you are likely to see. In fact it doesn't even hit his head. He leans into it and it bounces off his upper arm, but after the luck we've had at this ground in the past, Sunderland can hardly complain. In case you've forgotten, the words beach ball come to mind. Yes exactly.

The Redmen are in full voice when Gerrard plays an absolute peach of a pass to Sturridge who controls it superbly and squares for Mr Naughty to make it 2-0. Oh how the opposing fans love to hate young Luis and oh how he loves to ruin their day. The pantomime villain extraordinaire has done it again. Now it is at this point that we should be cruising but not us. As in every second half this season, it's as if Brendan and the backroom boys have been passing spliffs around to the players and putting treble whiskies in their half time tea. Predictably the Mackems pull one back which gives the home fans a massive boost. Mignolet who's been sound so far this season probably could've done better with a long shot but parries it out to the Italian lad Giaccherini and he pokes it home. I don't know why we do it. We just can't seem to play for the full 90 minutes.

A couple of close shaves when they nearly equalise are forgotten when we hit them on the break, and Daniel Sturridge sets up Suarez for the second time to finally put the game to bed. The fans, players and manager are all happy. Any away win in this league is a big win and our coach home will be a contended one. We're not there yet. I think we're playing to about 70% of our potential but going into the international break we'll be 2nd in the table and let's be honest, not many would've predicted that a month ago.

The journey home is the usual array of out of tune singing, slurred swearing and general misbehaviour. Amazingly the driver lives by me, so I skip town and get dropped about a mile away from our house. Hot Lips nearly falls off the couch when I walk in about 10.30pm for Match of the Day 2. This is what happens when you don't put a full pre-seasons worth of training in. You end up miraculously in your front room even earlier than you would've done if the match had been played at home. It's an astonishing turn of events. Hot Lips thinks I've been involved in some sci-fi time travel experiment but no, I just came straight home. I'll be on the Kop at the next game and people will be pointing at me going 'Isn't he the bloke who went straight home after the Sunderland game?' and his mate will be saying 'Yeah, that's him. What a lightweight. Oh, the embarrassment of it all.' All I can say is I promise it won't ever happen again.

Saturday 19th October 2013 – 12.45pm kick-off

Newcastle 2 Liverpool 2

I spent last weekend during the International break in Krakow, Poland in the company of some of my old bluenose mates. You may think that spending your free weekend with five bitter, blinkered, biased bluenosed bladder-headed buffoons when you're a cultured Redman would be hell on earth, but surprisingly it was just what the doctored ordered. A football free weekend with only a mild interest in England's match was the ideal pick-me-up. Obviously with Everton's very limited experience of European travel, I had to explain to them what passport control was and how to sit on an aeroplane the right way. Arguments were kept to a minimum as I tried to educate the novice half-wits without sounding too patronising. I think the poor dears fell for it.

Anyway, back to today, here I am sneaking around the house in the dark at 6am looking like a secret lemonade drinker. In the end I have to wake the dark mysterious one and ask her for a lift to the coach depot in Birkenvegas. Those bright summer mornings are but a distant memory as the dark unforgiving nights remind us that winter is on the way. I meet Parcel Parso who is so-called because he drives those big parcel lorries for Royal Mail and well, because his name is Parsons. He's not a mime artist or nothing, it's just his moniker. Dave Johno's there, as is Mugsy's lad, Dane, who's with his mate. We set off and pick up Ally, Ritchie, Mercer and Smigger from Scottie Road, and onto the last pickup at the Rocket in Broadgreen, then it's tally-ho all the way for this stupidly early kick-off time in Geordie-land. Big Phil, who is our leader, spokesperson, ringmaster and all-round trouble-shooter, makes his usual announcements at the front of the coach. We are told that we are going to stop at Chester-le-Street to restock the ale for the way home. So whatever you want for the return journey, get it now as we won't be stopping on the way back. "What! We're not stopping?" There's sideways glances all over the coach. He tells us to take all the empties off and get what we want for later so we can doss it in the luggage compartment. The troops are restless. He passes the Birkenhead suitcases (binbags) to every other seat and stipulates that not even a bottle top must be visible when we arrive by the ground, as the Geordie plod are the keenest in the country regarding the alcohol ban on coaches. "Yeah, but what about the stop off on the way back?" It's a big no. I don't know why, maybe it's John the driver, maybe people have got a do to go to? Who knows? But the bottom line is, no matter if we win, lose or draw, it's foot down and straight home after the game. This is a major blow for our little crew because that's the main reason we go on the coach. Besides the actual game, the stop-off is always the highlight of the day. If you're just going to bomb it there and bomb it back, you may as well drive and bin the car and have a bevvy in town.

Anyway, we make good time and arrive about an hour before the game and sneak over the road for a couple of liveners in The Black Bull. Jimmy McGill and Nocker, who are two of Liverpool's most famous doormen, stroll past. Now I'm not a great lover of the bouncer fraternity but these two have been part of my life as far as going out in town is concerned. They've looked after me, watched my back and beckoned me to the front of the queue for well over thirty hazy years.

From the ecstasy fuelled nuttiness of the State ballroom in the late eighties and early nineties, to the middle aged confusion of the last decade, those two have been there. I raise my glass to the pair of them in recognition. Outside the away end you have to go kind of underneath to the turnstiles. Now if you're ticketless and looking for an easy way to bunk in, here is my top tip for the day. Go past the first lot of entrances and to where the lift is, there's always a load of blaggers who can't be arsed walking up the ten or twenty flights of stairs to what is probably the highest away end in England. There's a few genuine limpers and asthmatics but there's also the fatties and the three toed sloths. Now if you head through to the lift they put your ticket bar code in a slot by the lift entrance but just ignore that and hang back. You are already past the turnstile bit if you've gone through for the lift, so just mingle and head up the stairs. It's a doddle but best achieved in the last fifteen minutes before kick-off. Whatever the weather, I am always here to help.

In the ground I speak to big Patto who's with Barry and Denise. He's been speaking to Tommy Press-Ups about his chemotherapy. With a bit of luck and a fair wind, he could be available for a Christmas drink at the Cardiff home game on the 21st. Nothing would please me more than to see the old mucker reunited with his off-field striking partner Danny Giles, before Christmas. Danny's missed him, you can tell. He's been trying to play upfront on his own against some very defensive bar maids, but with Tommy alongside him, he can open them up with some creative wit, wisdom and a little stupidity. Without Mr Press-Ups he's taking his chances too quickly. He's shooting on sight and sometimes missing the target by miles. In fact it's true to say that there's been a few red cards as well. Mainly for abuse and it's all down to frustration at missing the influence of his veteran strike partner. Who knows Danny might even go to the bar on his return. On second thoughts, maybe not.

The first half was a fairly open affair with Cabaye breaking the deadlock for them on 23 minutes. He picks the ball up around the centre spot and just keeps running at us. No-one is closing him down so he thinks 'don't mind if I do' and cracks one in from about thirty yards. Mignolet probably could've done better but to be honest, the defenders in front of him should've been more aware. It's not like he's never scored from long range before. We are getting a bit twitchy as half time beckons. But then Sturridge plays Suarez through on goal and Yanga Mbiwa pulls him down. Straight red and penalty. Stevie slots it and celebrates his 100th Premier League goal. A magnificent achievement from a true legend. People will tell you that Kenny was the greatest Red of all time. And everyone is entitled to their own opinion. But take it from me kids, I've watched nearly every game of both of their careers and Stevie is the No. 1. It's only when he retires from football that everyone will realise just how good he was.

We go in at 1-1 half time and the gents toilets are shrouded in mist. At every away game it's more or less the same. There are pockets of people puffing away on their ciggies as if their lives depended on it. But today was spectacularly smoky. To witness the grimacing faces of the non-smokers, as they fight through the fog, is a sight to behold. It's almost an exercise in who can pull the most disgusted face. An over-acting masterclass where the smokers celebrate a rare fifteen minute victory over the moral majority. Every oppressed part of society has their moment and if today's toilets tokers had been filmed, the title would be 'Lung Porn – The Smokers Revenge' certificate X.

Back in the fresh air of the real world our second half woes continue. Unbelievably after bracing ourselves for a hatful of goals in the second half against ten men, we concede to another suckerpunch setpiece. Their best player, Cabaye, crosses and some young lad called Paul Dunnett appears from nowhere and volleys home. It's his first goal and he's a local lad, so he's unsurprisingly overjoyed. We press and press and eventually Suarez links up well with Sturridge to provide him with an easy header for the equaliser. It's all one way traffic now but they hold out. Luis hits the bar with a peach of a volley which would've been goal of the season, but today is not our day.

Everybody's disappointed but it's not the end of the world, as all the teams this season seem to be dropping points here, there and everywhere. Yes we won 6-0 here last year but that was a freak result. Probably their worst defeat at home ever, so let's not get too down-hearted. Outside behind the line of stewards those fun-loving Geordie comedians give us a chorus of 'Feed the Scousers, don't they know it's Christmas time'. Well, actually it isn't Christmas time you thick Geordie half-wits. It's October the 19th and I've had quite sufficient to eat on the way here. And if I'm not mistaken I've got some chocolate Hobnobs as a treat on the way back.

The Angel of the North looks down on us as we head back in search of civilisation. The coach is a strange mixture of people of all shapes and sizes. The seat in front of us is occupied by big Dave and big Ted who defy the logic of physics to somehow remain seated together in such a small space for such a long journey. Their alcohol intake is absolutely frightening, which probably explains why they don't seem bothered about being shoe horned together. They just sing another duet, smile a nod of recognition and then get the bottle opener out and crack another couple of beers. Contented is what they are. Wee Claire, the unofficial coach mascot, who's sitting across the aisle from me is as far removed from Dave and Ted as is humanly possible.

She is the size of a family cat and must weigh roughly the same as a bag of sugar. There she is, week after week, wide eyed, taking it all in, the good, the bad and the ugly. She is as much part of this travelling roadshow as the loudest, opinionated tough guys and duckers and divers. Yes, there's a bit of swearing and the odd toxic fart to contend with, but where else in life are you gonna find such utter brilliant nonsense on a Saturday afternoon? You've got Gerrard behind us who has decided that from now on he will only speak in rhyming slang for the rest of his life. Pure comedy. Liverpool FC has a cast of thousands, each unique in their own way, but all with the same common goal of supporting the Mighty Reds in their ongoing quest for long overdue success.

We spill off the coach in London Road after dropping off at the Holt in Kenny and all go our separate ways. Our four go to the Victoria Cross for one last gargle. There's three bluenose mates in there who've just been to Castle Doom to see the Infidels beat Hull 2-1 in a match that Hull should've won. Usually I'd be shooting from the hip and giving them my usual volley of abuse but I'm struggling. I'm treading water. I need to get home. My work here is done. I make my excuses and disappear into the night.

Saturday 2nd November 2013 – 5.30pm kick-off

Arsenal 2 Liverpool 0

It's the Monday morning after the Arsenal match and I still feel a bit ropey. My head appears from under the duvet with the blank expression that is usually reserved for someone they have just pulled from the wreckage of a devastating earthquake; the miracle man who has survived for ten days under a collapsed building without food or water, looking dazed and confused. Well that's me right now. Ok maybe I'm exaggerating slightly because I've been quite comfy in my own bed but that's how I feel at the mo, absolutely done in. I've got mixed emotions about the weekend. On one hand I've thoroughly enjoyed myself. Had a great blow-out with all the characters that make up our legendary fan base. But on the other hand, and this is the reason that we disrupt our lives, our loves and our work patterns, the result. Yes, we've had a laugh, but the bottom line is we got beat. Many of you will say there's no shame in losing to Arsenal. They're top of the league. I understand that. But this was our first major test. We had done quite well. We had a little wobble against the Saints, beaten the Mancs but this was our first biggie away and we failed the test. I think I'll hibernate for a few days, then come up for air and re-evaluate the situation. Maybe a bit of healthy eating, five-a-day and all that, and I don't mean a vodka and orange, a gin and lemon and three bananas on the fruit machine. I mean the real stuff. I wanna have rosy cheeks like Kenny Dalglish. So it's a fitness regime and strictly no alcohol until Fulham at home on Saturday.

I had had a good vibe about this fixture all week. Sometimes as a footy fan you get a feeling and the Arsenal match was a good positive feeling. The only other loss this season was the Southampton defeat back in September. That day I walked into my local Ladbrokes to place the usual ridiculously hopeful bets and the friendly cashier CJ asked me for my prediction. I told him I had a feeling of impending doom and the boys in Red would lose one goal to nil. He said that all morning he'd been taking bets on four or five nil to Liverpool and that mine was the only negative voice he had heard. He asked me to put a bet on it but that would be blood money. How could I go in with my head held high and pick up my winnings. Not a hope in hell. But I just knew we would slip up.

Arsenal was the opposite. I really thought we were going to make some headway. Maybe go top. You may say I'm a dreamer, but I'm not the only one. We're all dreamers when it comes to supporting our team. In the week running up to the match it had become apparent that this was bigger than your average clash between these two historic rivals. The ticket situation was dire. Nobody had anything. I was already sorted but loads of regulars were pulling out as the price of travel and the lack of trains back made it dodgy to go all the way down there just on spec. Initially I was going to go with my mate Kev Sampson but that went pear-shaped. Then Parso had to work. Then I was going to try and do a hot shoe shuffle and just get on the train with Ritchie as he works for Virgin, but in the end I just had to bite the bullet and pay £78 fuckin' quid on an open-ended ticket. Add that to your £62 match ticket, plus this that and the other, and it works out at an eye-watering sum. What forced my thinking was Smigger who's been going to a few of the games with me this season phoned to say that playwright Dave Kirby had booked him on the train and they'd also sorted a Travelodge in Kings Cross, with the added bonus that I could dive in with them to save a bit of moolah. The only other viable option was to stay at Bucko's in Wembley. But that would involve negotiating a long tube journey whilst under the influence of alcohol, or arguing with immigrant taxi drivers about their imaginative price structure. And believe me, nothing pisses me off more than some little fuckin' chancer who can barely speak a word of English trying to charge me four times the price of what it really is. Trust me, I've driven taxis for more years than I care to remember and I know exactly how it works and what I'm on about. So Kings Cross it is then.

We meet at Limey and set off on the 10.48 which gets us to Londinuim for 1pm. Tage, who is Liverpool's unofficial King of Norway, is sitting across the aisle from us and entertains us with humorous stories about when he was Everton's interpreter for a match in Bergen a few years back. How he had to keep a straight face when he was told by the Everton representatives to tell the hosts that they were going to build a ground of 75,000 to rival Manchester United, and how Everton were the main club in the city of Liverpool. See, it's not just their fans who talk bollocks and have delusions of grandeur. It's also the incompetents who run the circus at Castle Doom. Tage is sitting there next to a lad called Liam, who I see at most aways. Always there through rain, hail or shine. But the thing that's different from say me or you, is that Liam is totally blind. He just gets up and wanders to the toilet and I'm thinking how does he know which side the toilets are on. How does he negotiate the tube or the crowds. It's amazing to watch. As he gets off the train and enters the great metropolis I think to myself, there for the grace of Robbie Fowler go

I. He's the type of person who should be winning Fan of the Year awards, far more deserving than some of our previous recipients.

We get off and head to the Travelodge at Kings Cross to check in. Whereas Dave and Smig put their bags on the bed and do that sit down and bounce thing that people do to test the mattress, I, on the other hand, stare down at the uninviting floor space by the window and accept that this might not be the most comfortable nights kip I'm ever going to have. But hey, I've slept in stranger places. Within ten minutes we're in The Friend At Hand pub by Russell Square tube station and the serious drinking is underway. This is big Keith's local and he is joined by his cousin big John Bankcroft. In fact, everyone seems to be big. Even big Chris from Brighton and his son big Harry are here. Big Chris doesn't like me calling him big Chris from Brighton. "Just cos I live in Brighton doesn't mean I'm from fuckin' Brighton. I'm from Kirkdale, born and fuckin' bred." Ok ok. Keep your hair on. It's only a figure of speech. Just when I'm beginning to feel dwarfed by Liverpool's large away following, I hear THE VOICE echo across the room. It's official. The Buck has arrived. Stand by your beds. It's almost like the diminutive Captain Buckley has come to inspect his troops. What he lacks in height he makes up for in sheer personality and charisma. Thank god there's a few smaller fellas coming in. For a few moments it felt like I'd got off the train from Lilliput Central into the Land of the Giants.

As the 5.30pm kick off time sneaks up on us, we decide to make tracks to the Emirates. I still can't get my head around the way English clubs prostitute themselves to foreign investors and allow their stadiums to be called after basically anything these days. I remember writing in my literary classic 'REDMEN – A Season On The Drink' that I'd be pissing my stripy pyjamas in some dodgy nursing home before the Liverpool Red Sox would run out at their new home, the Oman Go man Show man arena. Now obviously at the time I was just having a bit of fun and trying to be provocative, but little did I know, that spookily the owners of the Boston Red Sox would purchase our club from the previous pair of blood-sucking parasites. It just goes to show that nothing is sacred anymore and in five years' time we could well be running out at the ...., no I can't say it. Let me just stick my head down the toilet and flush. Ah, that's better.

Where was I? Oh yeah, we pile into the Emirates with dreams and songs to sing and the rest you will probably know. Cazorla hits the post with a header and rams home the rebound. 1-0 to the Gooners. Our midfield gets overrun and we are second best all first half. Suarez (he's not the Messiah, he's a very naughty boy) takes a quick free kick to Sturridge who squares it for Henderson to score, but no, referee Martin Atkinson decides he wants to book Sagna and makes us take the free kick again. Decisions, decisions. Half time comes and we head down the stairs looking for somewhere quiet so we can smoke ourselves to death undetected. Brendan Rodgers has seen enough of the hapless Cissokho and taken the Valencia loanee off and replaced him with Coutinho. It's his first game back after seven weeks out but he does ok. At least he can give the front two some much needed service. On the hour mark though, Aaron Ramsey tries his luck with a bit of a hit and hope. It flies in and that's that. There's no way we are coming back. Yes Suarez hits a post and yes he should have squared one to Sturridge instead of shooting, but at the end of the storm there was to be no golden sky. To be honest, we never looked like winning. We huffed and we puffed but we were never going to blow the house down. They were the better team so I don't think we can complain too much.

Listen to me, we can't complain too much. Of course we can

complain. I spend my whole life complaining. I don't think I've ever watched the red men get defeated and not complained. I want the best for us and every defeat hurts like hell. The day you don't feel pissed off by getting beat is the day to pack it all in. We adjourn over the road to The Drayton Arms where we all have a communal moan to get it off our chests. It's a kind of therapy to free ourselves up for the night ahead. You don't want to be having flash backs of Ramsay's twenty yarder when you're skipping the light fandango. There'll be enough time for post-match depression when you wake up with the hangover from hell tomorrow morning, and you're presented with the day's papers. Griffo and Pooley are in there with a mate who's a Director on ITN News. That's the type of company I'm keeping these days. You thought it was all bricklayers, spivs and wheeler dealers. No siree. I'm hanging with the big boys now. Not just the big fellas from the pub before the game, but people with a bit of pull. If only I didn't keep messing things up by telling all these influential people to fuck off, who knows where I'd be.

We sup up and march to The Garage venue up on Highbury corner where a Hillsborough fundraiser is taking place. It's a bit weird having a Liverpool function on the manor of the team you've just played. A bit like Arsenal having a do at the Sandon or somewhere by Anfield. Feels very strange. There's a door charge of fifteen quid to get in, which doesn't go down too well. So we dig our heels in and ask to speak to the organisers. There's a lot of walkie-talkie business going on with various door staff and stewards. But in the end I manage to get us all sorted with wristbands, and we make our entrance. It's not like we've never raised any funds for Hillsborough before. Most of us have spent the last twenty odd years plugging away to try and finance this long overdue justice. The justice that always seems to get plucked out of our grasp, just when it seems like it's in touching distance. Always so near, always so close, always another delay. One great day when all the prevarication is over, we'll get there.

John Power is leaving as we are going in, so we have missed his set, which leaves us with the longest auction of football memorabilia and other stuff that has ever been witnessed. And then the highly rated Tea Street Band to finish off. The auction drags on and on, with some fairly good prizes and some dubious compering. The two lads in the spotlight are clearly having the time of their lives, but it's a tough job to do, so we'll let them off for being a bit wahey! Finally after what seems like hours of waiting, the Tea Street Band appear from behind a fog of dry ice. A bit like the toilets at Newcastle the other week. Don't ask me what the songs were called or what they were about. It was just good. I really like them and would loved to have stayed until the end but that's when the incident happened.

Almost every match day following the Mighty Reds is punctuated by a moment that defines it from the others. Obviously the score is the first thing every fan remembers. But usually there is something so serious or stupid that six months later you'll remember it, for that reason and that reason alone. It all started when somebody, (probably Smigger), said to me, "So what happened to the famous lucky undies then? I thought we were supposed to win when you wore them." Then Clarkey and Luke and all their lot started to join in, saying that a lot of use they are and that you need to get rid and invest in a new pair. The lucky undies had let me and the team down, and drastic measures were required. I stormed off to the toilet, into the cubicle and removed what were once the Kop's coolest, luckiest undercrackers, and reappeared with them above my head, shouting "SACRIFICE. This is what you wanted brothers and sisters. Let the ritual begin." And with that, we set them on fire and I held the burning bills above my head for as long as humanely possible, then threw them to the floor as the tribal chanting got louder. "BURN, BURN, BURN". The trance-like frenzy wasn't like heavily moustachioed middle-eastern men burning the American flag. No, this was more of a ceremonial send off, a goodbye to the old and a space for a new beginning. Try telling that to the bouncers! They were swarming all over the place with serious intent and a lot of hand gestures, as the band played on. The suspects (us) were rounded up and asked to leave, which we did, with our heads held high. Ejected from a gig aged 55, 56 and 56 respectively. Sure we deserve some sort of badge or accolade. Thirty seconds from start to finish. Quite pleased with ourselves we decided to extend our stay in Highbury and found a boozer called the Hen & Chicks. I have vague memories of trying to dot the i's and cross the t's, for a couple of gunners in there, but by then I think we had already entered the twilight zone. Mysteriously zoomed back to Kings Cross by some unknown mode of transport, we reconvene with Luke, Clarkey and co. The Northumberland Arms, The Carpenters to the Travelodge bar and finally to the corner of an uninviting stretch of carpet on the hardest floor imaginable.

The next morning I feel like I've been pushed off the tallest building in London and landed here on the hotel floor. Miraculously I am still alive but I seem to be missing one pair of scarlet red boxer shorts. I try to trawl through the debris of what went on last night. Did I get kidnapped by Filipino nymphomaniacs who suckled on me like hungry piglets and who stole my undies as a trophy? Or hang on a minute…. It's all coming back to me now. SHIT. The HJC do at The Garage. Did we really get ejected for burning the …? Oh no, I hope we didn't look too silly. What will the organisers say? Perhaps they didn't notice. Oh god, beam me up Scottie and get me home. We enter Euston and the fuckin' bastard Liverpool train terminates at Crewe where there's a rail replacement service. Just what you need with a hangover that measures 7 on the Richter scale. Dave and Smigger make a snap decision to get the train to Manchester, and get one home from there. Me, I just walk off in a trance on my own and board the Crewe train, where I sit in the naughty corner staring into space. I phone Hot Lips ahead and beg for her to pick me up at Limey. I tell her about my little misdemeanour and being used to all the matchday madness and footy frolics, she just does that knowing voice and says "How old are you?" As I get off the bus by the Empire, I'm making my way round to the pick-up and drop-off point at the station when I have to do a double-take. On the main steps on the entrance of Lime Street, I see three girls in full view of everyone with their tits out being photographed. Taxi drivers are honking their approval, shoppers stop and stare. It may well be 2pm on a Sunday afternoon but the weekend can still throw up an unexpected surprise. If Bucko was here, he'd have a heart attack. Welcome to Liverpool.

Hot Lips is there on time. "Did you have a good weekend?" she says. "Yeah, it was alright. The usual. Nothing too mad." I said, lying through my teeth.

Saturday 23rd November 2013 – 12.45pm kick-off

Everton 3 Liverpool 3

I am feeling fresh and rejuvenated. Fit and healthy and ready to rock. I've just spent the international break sunning my stunning bar-room physique around the swimming pool in Tunisia. Just me and the long suffering Hot Lips. You could almost feel the envious eyes of other blokes gazing at my one-pack as I nonchalantly stroll around the sunbeds. I believe good old Ingerland played a couple of friendlies whilst I was out there, but I'm afraid I just couldn't be arsed watching either. I know one was against Germany but I've no idea who the other one was. I only knew they were playing because some of the hotel guests were sporting three lions tops to complement their array of haircuts, dodgy earrings and those horrible three quarter length below the knee shorts. I was kind of acting a bit aloof with mock surprise. Scousers always act a bit like they are the canine's testicles when they are on holiday. Always talking down to other team's fans like they are a sort of sub-species. I'd just finished telling my new mate Paul from Pontefract, Yorkshire, who was clad in his Leeds United shirt, that the proper hardcore Redmen don't go in for all of that shirt wearing nonsense. We like to be a bit more discreet. So feeling quite self-important, myself and Hot Lips leave the poolside and walk up to the room, and it's only then that she reminds me that a) there is a three foot liver bird on my towel, b) there was a liver bird on the bag that I put the towel in, and c) there is a liver bird tattooed on my upper arm. So here's me looking all smug thinking that I'm educating our nation's football fans, when in reality I'm walking back to the room looking like a cross between Bill Oddie and the birdman of Alcatraz on the way to a twitcher's convention. Liverpool fans, eh, what are we like. Discreet? We like to think so.

They're a strange species Evertonians. I've always likened them to the Scots with their obsessional dislike of all things English. Before a jock has even taken his tartan pyjamas off, and had his first spoonful of porridge, he's banging on about how everything that's wrong with the world is the English's fault. The Evertonians are no different. The Monday evening when Everton beat Newcastle I was in the pub and when the final whistle went, some lad in a blue shirt punched the air and the first thing he said was, "We're not far behind the red shite now. We'll catch those bastard Kopites up." I tapped him on the shoulder and said that I'd been on a coach to watch Liverpool the day before at Sunderland, and not one person on the entire bus coming home after our win had even mentioned the word Everton. "No need" I told him. It's a full time obsession they have trying to overthrow the Mighty Reds. The bottom line is they will always remain in our shadow, no matter what. He just looks at me like I'm mad.

It's been 12 years now since old skeletor (Moyes) said he thought Everton were the People's Club and 12 years on, I still have no idea what it means. Does it mean all the people support Everton? Obviously not, when you see that they haven't had an average gate higher than us in over 43 seasons. That's a long time in football. In fact it's more or less the whole of the modern era. Maybe they mean all the local people of Scouse heritage support Everton. Wide of the mark again. Go into any school on a kid's sports day and the red shirts outnumber the blues massively. Televised matches? Ask any licensee if they do more business when Everton are live than Liverpool, and the answer will be, of course not. Look around you at work, in the pub and on the street, it's a fallacy created by a fan base and an ex-manager who are desperate to give their club an identity. Moyes has left and the amiable Martinez has taken his place, but instead of righting this ridiculous piece of untrue marketing madness, what does Bill Kenwright and his band of directionless Directors do? They decide to paint in even BIGGER letters, the words Everton The People's Club, not only outside the ground but now all around the stands inside the bleedin' ground. Not only that, they have the other suspect slogan 'Born not manufactured' which obviously is a dig towards their more illustrious neighbours, implying that us Liverpool fans have somehow randomly stumbled across our calling late in life, whereas they were born a blue and people somehow decided to support the world's greatest club as an afterthought. How horribly wrong they are. The cheeky cheeky blue-nosed bastards. This is why, contrary to popular belief amongst our worldwide fanbase who sometimes think that Manchester United are our number one rivals, this is the one. The derby match will always be number one. Nobody enjoys getting beaten by United, but defeat against these twats is nigh on unbearable. We share our daily lives, whether we like it or not, in the company of Evertonians. And when they win, every couple of years or so, it is worse than any other defeat. It's Everton away today. Let's just do the business and get it out of the way. Come on Redmen. Let battle commence.

As usual it's an early kick-off and as usual, hardly anyone has got tickets. I have a ring around and persuade Parso, who's the world's greatest worrier, to accompany me to the ground in search of the elusive, lesser-speckled derby ticket. He's a cracking lad Parso, but he does panic somewhat. His epitaph, when it's all said and done, should be 'what if'. We get to The Twelfth Man about an hour before the game and I score a ticket off someone straight away. It's not a fluke as I've fired over twenty texts out. Parso's face looks nervous. He's getting twitchy and probably thinking 'he's dragged me out of my comfort zone to come here, and now he's got a ticket, I'm gonna be discarded outside the ground while he goes in and has a great time'. Not so fast Mr Parsons, as another of my irons in the fire ignites. Right, that's us sorted. I'm just taking a self-satisfying sip of my pint in the pub doorway when BANG, a huge firework goes off outside. I chip my tooth on the pint glass I'm drinking from with shock. We look outside and there's a fairly big group of young urchins who are obviously in the mood for a bit of a rumble with their Everton counterparts. I don't know how they can tell who's who, as they all look the same to me. It's a bit like having a fight with your own mirror image. I've always found it a bit weird, Liverpool and Everton fans beating the shit out of each other after the derby. Surely there's bigger fish to fry, as Scousers are hardly the most loved species of British sub culture. We've always been looked down upon by the rest of the nation as some fiercely independent republic populated by agitators, loveable rogues and rough diamonds. Maybe there's a hint of truth in that assessment, so surely it would make more sense to stand together, united instead of inflicting serious injury on neighbours, workmates and blokes who drink in the same pub as you.

Maybe I'm just being a bit idealistic as I get older, because when I was their age I was probably just as bad. The only difference was that back then even though there was a huge amount of hooliganism at the games, Liverpool and Everton never fought. There was always little fall-outs and isolated incidents but on the whole both sets of hoolies knew each other and would join up when one team played another team with a bit of a reputation. It was almost like the city of Liverpool versus the rest of the world. Sadly now the blues and the reds are divided and yet again, like every other derby, there will be trouble. Not on a grand scale but trouble nonetheless. Me and Parso skirt Stanley Park and walk past The Abbey pub as Castle Doom comes into sight. There's always the slight feeling of butterflies as we approach the Bullens Road side of the ground. I think that's just the fear of defeat that's hovering subconsciously around your mind. Nobody wants to be on the losing side in a derby. The bluenoses are used to it but we're certainly not. When we suffer our one defeat every three or four years, it absolutely kills me. It takes weeks to recover. It's almost like having an illness caused by football. In fact if you went to the doctor, he'd probably just say that you had a bad case of the blues, with the only known cure being a convincing win the next time you play them.

We're in the queue outside the ground and there's a face next to me that I recognise. Well if it isn't Mr Jamie Carragher as I live and breathe hanging out with the lads. Don't you just love 'im? He could easily be poncing about in some corporate hospitality lounge in the main stand but no. He's queuing up outside the away end in his hooded coat just like any other expectant fan. Well in Jamie lad. A true ledge.

The game itself is an absolute stormer. Probably THE best ever. The pundits, the players and the journos reckon it's the best since the 4-4 at Castle Doom in 1991. Take it from me Redmen this was far superior. Back then we battered Everton with four great goals but undid all our good work with four sloppy mix-ups in our area. This now in 2013 is a far more accomplished Everton who haven't lost at home in the whole of 2013. Two evenly matched teams going at it hammer and tong for 90 pulsating minutes. The Evertonians have waited years to see their team play with a freedom and confidence that David Moyes had kept stifled under a blanket of caution and paranoia. This was always going to be an open game. But the sheer intensity and non-stop action was mesmerising. James Pearce of the Liverpool Echo described it like watching two heavyweights desperately trying to deliver the knock-out blow but leaving themselves wide open to attack. There was joy, relief, pride, frustration and a sense of injustice. This was a game Liverpool should've won but came very close to losing. You couldn't take your eyes off it for a second.

The two biggest talking points for the Reds were the outrageous x-rated tackle on Suarez in the first half by Kevin Mirallas. A hundred per cent sending off offence, which unbelievably only got a yellow. Absolutely no intention of playing the ball. There were stud marks across Suarez's thigh and yet Mirallas is allowed to carry on and influence a second half of which he should've been watching from the stands. Most players would've been happy to wave goodbye from a stretcher after a tackle like that, but not King Luis. He just gets himself back on his feet and is even more passionate, if that's at all possible. As Rodgers commented afterwards, if the tackle was the other way round and Suarez committed the foul, there would only be one scenario. A red card and a lengthy ban. That's the second slice of luck they've had concerning Suarez in the last two years. His winning goal here a year ago was chalked off by the officials for no apparent reason.

The other talking point, and the one which kept getting repeated deep into the night in the pubs and clubs, time after time, was how the fuck did Joe Allen miss that? It's fair to say that Joe will not have had the best night's sleep he's ever had after that. And yes, it was a howler. It would've put us 3-1 up with half an hour left, but even that wouldn't have been water tight today. It was that sort of a match. Then we had Jon Flanagan playing his first derby game getting the Man of the Match with a faultless display, playing out of position at left back. Mignolet in goal, making some exceptional saves at vital moments, and Coutinho and Suarez giving us that South American flair. A quick run down of the goals: long corner from Gerrard finds Coutinho at the far post, bang, 1-0 on five minutes; Ross Barkley nods down to the Mirallas, 1-1 eight minutes gone; Barry fouls Suarez twenty-five yards out, he picks himself up and curls an absolute beauty around the wall and into the Gwladys Street net, get in there! There's only nineteen minutes on the clock and it's 2-1 to us already. The score somehow stays the same until half time. Even the fans needed to catch their breath during this fifteen minute break. It's back upstairs and Everton are really piling on the pressure. Mignolet is having a blinder but can do nothing to stop Lukaku from equalising for the bitter blues. It's end to end stuff. Howard saves brilliantly from Suarez's header but with eight minutes left, Lukaku again loses his marker and nods home from a corner. I fall to my knees. There are few worse feelings in the world, than your bitterest rivals scoring the winner in the last few minutes. Castle Doom is rocking. The infidels think they've done it. My head is banging. My heart is racing. My fingernails are disappearing. Nervous faces glance all around. As Gerrard swings a cross in from the right, Daniel Sturridge, who's only been on the pitch the last ten minutes, rises above everybody and heads it home. GERRINDER!!! YES. YES. YES.

The whistle goes on the greatest derby in living memory. Nobody knows what to say or think. Of course we could've won it. But so could they. You would never in a million years hear an Evertonian say it, but I will. It was a fair result. A great game played at break neck speed by two open attacking teams.

Me and Parso walk back to The Twelfth Man through the crowds who cannot believe what they have just witnessed. Everyone has their own opinion where it could've been won or lost. We just need a drink. A big drink. The pub is ridiculously packed, even moreso than a home game. We only have a couple then head off into town. For the first derby in over a decade, we don't go to Ned Kellys (The Victoria Cross) for a drink. It feels a bit weird as it's been HQ for years, especially for the big games. The Picture House is full of the old school over-40 reds. Terrace legends like Tony Gill, Fat Eddie, Mick Duffy, even little Evo from Halewood makes a cameo appearance. There's Doyley and Kenno and there's Degsy from Aigburth. In fact I could probably name half the pub, so I'll stop right there. We head to Ma Edgies then to the Yankee Bar which is scally central, and far too noisy and boisterous to relax, so we slope off to some of the less manic watering holes, where we can at least sit down and talk. It's not really an age thing, it's just that I've been standing up for about nine or ten hours and we're all flagging. I text the blue noses to tell them the city, as usual, is all red. The lightweights have already departed the town centre and are probably in their blue and white striped pyjamas ready for Match of the Day, when a text off me old mate TC, the bluenosed reprobate comes through. 'Great game mate. Probably a fair result. We all got off an hour ago.' Well knock me down with a feather. Never in all my born days has one of the most blinkered, biased, bitter bluenoses ever said after a derby match, that it was a fair result. Think about it, an Evertonian actually saying it was a fair result. It just doesn't ring true. He's obviously had his phone hacked or been abducted by aliens.

No Evertonian is rational or humble or gracious, so I'm afraid I'll have to phone him in the morning to get confirmation of this extraordinary ground breaking statement. This could be front page material for Monday's Echo. Imagine the headlines. EVERTON FAN NOT ANGRY SHOCK. EVERTON FAN IN FAIR ASSESSMENT BOMBSHELL. EVERTON FAN ENJOYS DERBY MATCH. BITTER BLUE HAS NO COMPLAINTS. There would be riots down County Road as his fellow Toffees begin to tear up their 'half-season' tickets in disgust at one of their own for speaking out in a non-confrontational manner. "How could he" they cry. How could he say such things in a measured, rational way. It's been a strange and yet enjoyable derby day. One of the best. But it's gonna be hard to sleep because I'm still puzzled by the 'fair result' text. Could the world have gone completely mad?

Sunday 1st December 2013 – 2.05pm kick-off

Hull 3 Liverpool 1

In the week running up to this fixture, the city of Hull, much to everyone's amazement was awarded the title of UK City of Culture 2017. Let me just repeat that for you. Hull, UK City of Culture… Now I know what you're thinking, you're probably just sitting there looking completely blank. In fact, you may have even stopped thinking and gone into a trance like state. Well snap out of it and let's look positive here. A little experiment may be needed. Put the book down and close your eyes, and begin to mutter the words Hull, Hull, Hull under your breath for five minutes. Think of all the amazing cultural gifts that this great city of Hull has bestowed on this grateful land of ours. On completing this task you may wish to share your thoughts and observations. Or on the other hand, you may be a bit like myself, scratching your head thinking how the f***, who the f*** and why the f***. Now I know I'm sounding a little bit critical here seeing as Liverpool was knocked in some quarters as being a bit too rough and ready when they were awarded the European Capital of Culture. But fuck me, we were talking about Liverpool then. BIG BAD INDEPENDENT LIVERPOOL with culture oozing out of every pore. I mean what is culture. I would say music, sport, the arts, history and architecture. So what would Liverpool put forward as evidence. Music, the Beatles, biggest band ever in the history of popular music bar none. Sport, Liverpool FC, one of the most famous and successful and best supported teams in world football. The Arts, Tate Modern and the Walker. History, the place is crawling with it, second biggest port of the British Empire. Architecture, more listed buildings than anywhere else outside London. That's culture for you. Which brings me back to dear old Hull. I don't know what the criteria was for this strange, unexpected decision. I was a big fan of the Housemartins / The Beautiful South back in the day, but even they would be the first to admit that they hardly changed the face of worldwide popular music culture. I even went online to see if I'd missed something but no. There's fuck all there that any other run of the mill sized town has got or could do. If you delved deep enough and put together a portfolio of anywhere, you could easily surpass it. Birkenhead for instance, on the face of it, just a crusty old punch drunk working class town, but give me a day or two and I could produce a brochure of amazing facts, figures and things of beauty that would piss all over the City of Culture 2017. So what's happened here is this, they've thought right who needs a leg up, who's struggling a bit and could do with a makeover and could do with a couple of bob to resurrect their ailing fortunes. I know, Hull. They're pretty crap. We could put a bit of lipstick on the mouth of the Humber and see how we can seduce the gullible. So this is how it will work. They'll probably get a new theatre. A few bands and comedians will tour there. Some of the cafés and bars will put seats outside and a few Southern media types will come up to drink all the white wine and see if they can get their snouts in the trough for any funding. Then 2018 will come and when the hangovers have cleared, everybody will wake up and discover without it's make up on, it's still unremarkable Hull.

Right, I think I've said enough regarding our host city of today's match. Maybe I was a little harsh, but hey a little piss taking of your match day rivals has always been part and parcel of the game. And also quite therapeutic. We stop off in the groovy town of Howden about twenty miles away, where the entire coach invades the Working Mens Club, while our lot sneak round the corner to The White Horse for a few thirst quenchers. With it being a Sunday game it's not as busy as when we've been here in the past, but it's the perfect stop-off for a pre-match gargle.

We arrive refreshed and ready for the first of three really winnable games. This one, Norwich at home on Wednesday and West Ham at home on Saturday. Should be a piece of piss. Should be, but this is Liverpool we are talking about here. And things don't always go to plan. We arrive at the wonderfully named K C Stadium and no, I don't know what it stands for either. I could probably look it up and reveal what the mysterious K C stands for, but I really can't be arsed. I know that as a writer I am supposed to furnish you with all the relevant facts, figures and information but I don't think any of us are really that bothered. In fact, in nearly all of these away games that I have described, there is one common thread that continually runs through the book. That is the actual lack of match action and boring stats. The aim is to tell you how we got there, who we went with, what happened and why on earth we do it. If you want in-depth match punditry and analysis, I can't help you. If you want to know who got a yellow card, or who was subbed on 51 minutes, you are reading the wrong account. This is just a tale of a season of away games, marinated in alcohol, song and camaraderie.

We are in the ground awaiting kick-off but we seem to have stumbled into a sort of political rally. The whole place is alive with angst and protest banners. It feels a bit weird like we've just gatecrashed someone else's party. The travelling Kop are trying their best to be heard but are drowned out by some very unhappy locals. The reason for all this disquiet stems from their Egyptian owner who, like nearly all of the foreign owners in the Premier League, seems to think he can just dismiss a club's tradition and change the club's name after a hundred and nine years. Mr Assem Allam thinks he's bought a basketball team. He wants to call Hull City, Hull Tigers, or is that Hull Tigers Kingston Rovers City or whatever. But the thing which has really sent the locals doolally was when the owner told the 'City till we die' action group, that they could all die as soon as they want. And that anyone who protests against him is a hooligan, because it's his club. When in reality it's their club and their community. Yes the business fraternity will say that he owns it and he can do what he wants with it, but football is unique. Your team is your town and those fans will be there long after Mr Allam has departed to fund his next ego-driven venture. It's like that creepy little cartoon character down at Cardiff. He's even worse with his replica shirt pulled badly over his shirt and tie, looking like a James Bond baddie. That shady little greaseball has decided that the bluebirds are no longer blue anymore. No, he's decided that Cardiff are now the reds, because it's his lucky colour. Fuck tradition, fuck what the players and fans think. Mr Vincent Tan, like a drunk in a sandpit, thinks that Cardiff City is his own personal playground. He may as well get up on the roof of the stadium, drop his kecks and piss on the fans heads below. It's like us playing in blue next season or saying to an Evertonian, sorry about this you bitter blues but from next year, it'll be you who'll be known as the red shite. It's all a bit mad and if the Premier League had any bollocks, they'd sort this type of behaviour out once and for all. But don't hold your breath because the spineless yes men in the corridors of power will just quietly cash the cheques under the KEEP CALM AND CARRY ON poster on the office wall.

Anyway, I believe there's a match today and against this backdrop of unrest the boys in red are absolutely awful. Some of the players think they can just turn up and the result will automatically go in our favour. How they can't be motivated is beyond me. I was up for it. I was out of bed at 6.30am. The whole coach was up for it. But this was dismal stuff, beaten for the first time in our history by whatever they are called, Hull something or other. The thing that does your head in most was that this was no freak result. It wasn't a smash and grab and then backs against the wall job. Far from it. They just got stuck in and wanted it far more than a very poor Liverpool team. Sturridge had done his ankle in in training, so he was missing and will be out for another two months. But we should be twatting teams like this, with or without certain players. Victor Moses on loan from Chelsea was atrocious. Time after time he gave it away or miskicked. Glen Johnson, usually so gifted, played like he was stoned or drunk, beaten to every 50/50 ball, he gave the impression that he really didn't want to be there. Sterling seems to have gone backwards. He started last season with rave reviews but on his first start of the season here, he flopped badly. Jake Livermore scored for them on twenty minutes after a really shit attempt at a flick by Moses. It was actually an own goal by Skrtel, but if Martin was worried about getting his name on the score sheet, he needn't have, because he scored another three minutes from the end, to put the final nail in Liverpool's coffin, on an afternoon to forget. It finished a painful 3-1 defeat with Gerrard scoring ours direct from a free kick and Meyler scoring their second, after another mix up in our box. This was the equivalent of our defeat at Stoke on Boxing

Day last year, or the hiding we suffered at St Mary's in Southampton, also last season.

We trudge out of the ground for the journey home, knowing that we could've been right up there with Arsenal, if we'd have won. But the cold hard facts are, we're not up there and we didn't win and it's a crap Steve Bruce team again that has foiled us. As usual the coach home after the defeat is full of irrational and outlandish arguments. Some valid, some just pure nonsense. But every match-going diehard is familiar with this type of behaviour. It's basically a lot of fans, who really care, letting off a bit of steam. But Brendan Rodgers will know that what we have seen today is totally unacceptable for Liverpool Football Club. We've got two home games coming up against two teams who we should normally batter, and anything less than two convincing wins and heads will drop. We must get ready to go again.

The coach pulls up on London Road and I'm delighted that the great Danny Giles and his sidekick the lovable Muffa Murphy are there to meet us in Ally's pub. It's mad Danny doesn't go to the aways so I can't take the piss out of him in this book. And Smigger doesn't go to the homes, so although they both follow the reds, they never really meet up. It's as if they're on different shifts at the same factory. It's a great end to a long and trying day. We have a couple in the Picture House round the back of the Empire to Ma Edgies onto the Yankee Bar which is packed full of urchins and far too noisy for surreal conversations and heated debate. So we move onto the Blob on Charlotte Street to drink Aussie Whites and talk shite. The last throw of the dice is the Globe opposite Central Station where I see an opening and I go for it. A little shimmy and I'm out of the pub, over the road and onto a train within minutes. I put the key in the door of

Dodd Towers and the Dark Mysterious One greets me with "I've recorded Match of the Day for you." I say thanks but tell her that I would rather eat my own flesh than watch that utter crap again. "Ah you must've got beat then" she says. "Oh you can read me like a book" I sarcastically reply, and then drop my cheese on toast face down on the carpet. It's just one of those days. Time for bed.

Saturday 15th December 2013 – 4pm kick-off

Tottenham Hotspur 0 Liverpool 5

After the miserable capitulation at Hull a fortnight ago, we needed to get back on track immediately. So two quick convincing wins at home seem to have steadied the ship. Suarez banged four beauties in against Norwich in a 5-1 win. Then we hammered the Hammers 4-1 on Saturday, so we are back in the mix, but tougher matches lay ahead. Our next three aways are Spurs, City and Chelsea. If we get a win and maybe one draw, I'll be delighted. Anyway, it's off to Tottenham on the 10.38 from Lime Street to a place where we've been beaten on all six of our last meetings. As usual, like any group of travelling fans, we discuss the forthcoming match with a mixture of outlandish optimism and negative doomed to fail resignation. Deep down though we are all the same. We all live in the hope that this could be the one. The special type of match where something amazing happens and you were there to witness it. Unfortunately there have been far too few of these types of games over the last twenty years. Europeans yes, Premier League no. We've had our moments on the road in England, most notably Man U away a few years ago when we tonked those odious bastards 4-1. The Newcastle six-niller was also a pleasure to watch, but I can't think of too many halcyon days down here in North London to cherish. I've been making the journey down here since the 1970's when my cow's lick stood proud, my bum fluff moustache failed and my teenage spots were in full bloom. In all my years of getting chased up the Seven Sisters Road, in trousers that were so wide I could've smuggled people into the ground in them, I don't remember us ever beating Spurs convincingly. Yes, there's been one-nils and two-nils, but we've never really mullered them at White Hart Lane. All that was about to change.

Ritchie, Merce, Smig and me are met off the train by Captain Bucko and making his debut at a Liverpool away game, my German nephew Joel, who has only been living in Londinium for about six months. He's a top lad Joey, chef at some fancy gaff in Islington, where he rustles up treats for the metropolitan chattering classes. Little does he know what he is about to witness in a few hours' time. In fact, little do we know what lays in store for us, as we tackle our first few pints of what will become a momentous day. We have to leave Russell Square to meet Cliffy Keogh and his mates in the big Wetherspoons by Liverpool Street station. Cliffy, who is a top lad, has one of the biggest and best smiles this side of the Mississippi. Off the top of my head, if I had to liken him to anyone, it would be Bingo out of the Banana Splits. If any of our younger readers are puzzled by what Banana Splits is, it was a mad programme years ago. Google it. We get off at White Hart Lane and walk through some kind of housing estate and up to the ground. We are in the crowded lower part of the away end which seems to have two people for every seat. The atmosphere is starting to simmer away nicely until suddenly it comes to the boil in the 18th minute. It's that man Suarez again, controversially made captain for the day in the absence of Gerrard and Agger. He latches onto Henderson's pass and buries it into the corner. Our end celebrates like only they know how. The most talked about player in English football has done it again. He really is a one off. I've seen them come and I've seen them go from this great club of ours. Many flatter to deceive. They arrive with huge price tags around their necks and fail to deliver. This fella is a proper street footballer. He plays as if it's his last day on earth. His passion, desire and pure will to win set him apart from the modern day stereotype of lazy, overpaid, arrogant footballer who is more interested in having the right haircut and diamond earring than having the right attitude. Opposing players must look at him in the tunnel before the game and think 'oh fuckin' 'ell, not him again'. They probably have sleepless nights just at the very thought of him. We may only have the pleasure of him for another year but we must enjoy it while we can, for we are in the company of a genius, along with Messi and Ronaldo, one of the top three players on the planet. On the opposite end of the scale Jordan Henderson has had criticism thrown at him from all sides for about two years. He could've gone to the mighty Fulham in the summer but stayed on to fight for his place. This was his moment. His best game in a red shirt and the match where he finally announced his arrival as a top midfielder. He absolutely bossed the game in Gerrard's absence. Maybe when Stevie plays he feels obliged to give it to the captain every time, instead of having to think for himself. Who knows. Anyway Hendo volleys home the second after two great saves from Lloris, the goalie. First from Hendo himself, next from Luis and finally Jordan puts us two nil up with five minutes to go till half time. Downstairs at the break there's an excited buzz about the place. The same faces that slumped out of the K C Stadium a couple of weeks ago, looking like they'd been to their own funeral, have come alive again. Vinnie and his mate, Charlie the doorman from The Twelfth Man, look like the happiest boys in town. Stef comes over and says she wishes the ref would just blow for full time now, so we can get the three points and get out of here. That type of caution comes from years of watching the reds and knowing how quickly things can go pear shaped. She needn't have worried though because things were only going to get better. Much much better.

With half an hour left Paulinho gets red carded for leaving his studs in Suarez's chest. I forgot to mention that Sakho has hit the post with a header when he really should've buried it and Coutinho has hit the bar with a cheeky dig in the first half. Then the defining moment in the match happens. With sixteen minutes remaining, Henderson back heels to Suarez who crosses it to young Jon Flanagan who absolutely twats it into the roof of the net. Complete and utter pandemonium ensues in the visitors section, as the players have a mass pile on in front of us. My glasses fly off into orbit over people's heads, as the mayhem takes hold. It's as if they're in slow motion disappearing into the crowd. As any glasses wearer knows, this could be a major problem if they're lost or smashed. There's people with torches on phones scouring the floor. Then after what seems like ages but probably only two minutes, some hero about four rows down holds them aloft. Thank fuck for that. The arms on them are a bit skew-whiff and they don't sit right but hey, I don't mind looking like some nutter you see hanging around a city centre bus station, as long as the Redmen get the win.

But it's not over yet folks. Not by a long shot. As the travelling army of fans go through the full repertoire of toe-tapping classics, Suarez is put through by substitute Alberto, and chips the goalie like only Luis knows how. I feel like I'm dreaming. This is total domination at a ground where we always struggle. Then just on full time as the seconds tick away, in front of a half empty stadium that man Suarez sets up Raheem Sterling to put the final nail in the coffin of AVB's Premier League managerial career. Oh happy days. The plan now, like last season, is to meet Bucko and go and have a few bevvies, with all the old Tottenham lads. But unlike most seasons when Spurs have celebrated their annual home win, this is different. We have just demolished their beloved team and Smigger reckons it could be a mistake to go behind enemy lines. Even though it's been fairly safe the last few years, they're going to be well and truly pissed off. And you only need one who doesn't think it's such a good idea to have about ten gurning Scousers in their midst trying to stifle their complete and utter joy. We decide to err on the side of caution and do the long walk to Seven Sisters tube.

It's absolutely pissing down. My socks are wet through. My coat is soaking. But in my heart it's sunshine all the way. It's amazing the effect football can have on you. It's like we're skipping through a flower filled meadow in spring. But in reality we're in a torrential downpour in a place that has seen serious unrest and rioting in the not so distant past. It's pointless Joel coming back to Euston with us, so we part at the tube station. I assure him that not all away games are as good as this. In fact, none of them are as good as this. He's had a great day, as we all have. I'm just glad that we've shared a pivotal moment together. He disappears down the escalator with dreams and songs to sing, now officially part of this great travelling circus that is Liverpool FC on the road. It's all well and good watching on a TV screen in a far foreign land but to experience the power of LFC amongst the celebrating hordes and to actually smell and feel the pure emotion of victory from under the floodlights at an away game will live with you forever. Joel Birkenholtz, welcome to the mad house.

We get to Euston and phone Ritchie to see if he's having a pint. He tells us there's a train leaving in fifteen minutes. We dive into Marks & Sparks and get four bottles each and meet Ritch and Merce in first class. A first class end to a first class day. We get off at Limey and bother Les Battersby who's at the bar in Ma Edgies. He's doing panto at the Empire and probably doesn't need us taking the piss out of him, after a hard day treading the boards. Oh yes he does. Oh no he doesn't. He's behind you, etc, etc. You get the gist. Muffa and Dougie appear from nowhere, as does Maddo. We all pile over to the Picture House to see Ally where he basically just shuts up shop, tills up and comes with us to a very lively Yankee bar. I leg it to Central to get the last train at twenty to twelve. It's been an absolute beast of a day. One of the best I can remember. We've put a massive statement and put down a marker for the rest of the season. Let's hope that this is the start of great things for this team of ours. Sleep tight Tottenham fans and don't have too many nightmares.

Thursday 26th December 2013 – 5.30pm kick-off

Manchester City 2 Liverpool 1

We're on a bit of a run at the moment. Since the Hull game, we've won 5-1, 4-1, 5-0 and last week at home we saw off new boys Cardiff with at 3-1 win. In fact, after our last two wins managers AVB of Spurs and Malky Mackay of Cardiff have both been sacked, which just goes to show what a cut-throat business this modern football is. The cartoon baddie Vincent Tan is the epitome of what is wrong with football these days, the archetypal mad millionaire who looks like he got dressed in the dark, is not just Cardiff's problem, he is football's problem.

Today's opponents, Manchester City, are arguably the richest club on the planet at the moment. But it wasn't so long ago in the not so distant past, that they were plying their trade in the lower divisions of English football. Playing in the third tier at away grounds where their dwindling band of fans would find solace with a cup of Bovril from a desolate caravan at the back of a windswept away end. A play-off win in 1998 against those giants of European football, Gillingham, gave them hope of a return to not exactly glory days, but at least the chance to compete at a higher level again. They then moved out of their Maine Road ground and took up residence in the City of Manchester stadium, which had been built for the Commonwealth Games. Before you knew it some oil rich Arab speculators had appeared from behind the sand dunes and completely transformed Manchester's much maligned underachievers into probably the most powerful, overpaid squad in the world. And that's where we are going today folks.

Whoever said football's a funny old game wasn't joking. This team have won every home game this season so far and are everybody's favourites to win the title. Our mission is to carry on our form into this match and have a right good go at them and see what happens. The performance like we saw at Spurs would be ideal but, with me being a veteran of over forty years of following this club of ours, I can safely say that the White Hart Lane massacre was a one-off and should be looked upon as such. Games like that come once every blue moon and talking of blue moons, it is the blue moonies who we aim to beat today.

It is a different type of away day today for the simple reason of it being Boxing Day and there being no public transport, so I gladly accept the offer of a lift from an old mate called Bob Bridge, who lives in Wallasey and can pick me up right outside Dodd Towers. We join another car load in Bebington by Tranmere's ground and do the short journey down the M53 and into Manchester on the M56. The other car consists of Nobby, Foz and a father and son team who live in Bristol. They take us to their usual City boozer but like loads of others these days, it's boarded up. We walk slightly away from the ground and into the most dodgy run down pub I've been to in years. And boy have I been in some iffy looking boozers in my time. It's called The Bank of England and looks as if it's been closed for fifty years, and opened especially for today's match with the opposite of a refit. I can't imagine what those Tripadvisor busy bodies would make of it, if they every dared to darken its doors. There's a couple of bouncers on the door who ask us if we're City, to which we mumble something along the lines of yes. It's obviously home fans only so for the first couple of rounds or so, we are conscious of not attracting attention to ourselves. I whisper to the barmaid, "three pints of lager and two Guinness please love" in a kind of mellow undistinguished north western accent, which I'm hoping comes across as a kind of Warrington, St Helen's type of lilt, but probably sounds more like a cross between Botswana and Papua New Guinea, with a hint of speech impediment thrown in for good measure.

We were doing well at keeping a low profile until the scores of the earlier games started flashing up on the pub screen. Everton nil, bottom club Sunderland one, is greeted with probably a little bit too much exuberance from our corner of the pub, which in turn raises the suspicion and eyebrows of some of our more shady Mancunian hosts. A culmination of an impromptu police visit and some noise from the other side of the pub throws them off our scent and within an instant, we are out into the cold dark street and up to the ground.

I meet Dadger and Ritchie and decide to squash in with them for the game. It's a bit packed but I'd rather be with mates than stuck on my own next to some tourist who just wants to take photos all match. The match is a corker. It's end to end stuff packed with incident. Already this season City have put six past both Arsenal and Spurs and four past United here, but for long periods of this match, we were by far the better team. Coutinho swept the Reds into the lead on 24 minutes after good work from Sterling. Then came the turning point of the match when Raheem Sterling scored the second only to be flagged for offside, when he was clearly three yards on. A decision described later by the manager as horrendous. These are the tiny details which Rafa used to go on about a few years ago. It's a clear goal. There's not even a debate to be had. We should've been two nil up but instead of having the luxury of a two goal cushion, where we could probably pack the midfield and hopefully see out the game. It's one nil and then we concede from a set piece again, as Kompany outjumps Skrtel to equalise. We need to get to half time to reorganise and take stock, but no, no, no. Just on the whistle Negredo is set free on the counter attack and kind of mis-hits his shot with the outside of his boot and Mignolet makes a right hash of it and palms it into his own net. Heads drop as the ref blows for half time. We've shot ourselves in the foot again. We should've won here last year until the much loved Pepe Reina had a rush of blood and fucked up for them to equalise late on. It's a cruel, cruel game.

The second half is a game played at breakneck speed with nothing going our way. Lescott goes right through Suarez on the edge of the box. Nothing. Near the end Lescott pulls Suarez's shirt in the area to stop him jumping. Nothing. It's so frustrating. We've played really well today against a very good City team. In terms of possession and chances we probably edged it but that means nothing in the cold light of day. The score in tomorrow's papers will read City 2 Liverpool 1. Outside the ground the City fans are bouncing. They know how important this win for them was and how easily they could've lost. Anyway it's head down and try and find the car. Usually I've got a built in homing device but for some reason we have a malfunction. Trying to be clever I'd taken a short cut through an estate and then completely lost my bearings. I managed to find the boarded up pub that we first went to but then had to phone for assistance. Bob, who is of an unflappable disposition just calmly says "Don't move, I'll be there in two minutes." Within a minute I'm in the car and we're off. The others had obviously left already. Normally when you get a bit lost your mates give you hell. "Where the fuck have you been? We've been waiting for ages, blah, blah, blah." But Bob, no. Cool as a cucumber but drives like a maniac. The way he negotiates the Manchester ring road you'd think we'd just pulled off one of the biggest bank jobs in history.

Less than an hour later, we're back on home territory making light work of some heavy drinking. The pubs are rammed. There's people dancing, the bands are playing. There's faces you haven't seen for years. They're looking at you as if to say "fuck me, he's starting to look old." And you're thinking "Fuck me he's starting to look old, where's all his hair gone" and "blimey that's some ale gut he's got there. Looks like he's scored a hat-trick and hid the ball up his jumper." There's people who come up and shake hands and do that insincere hugging thing and more drinks get drunk and more shite is talked. Then in the distance, amongst all the drunken revelry you hear the chime of the last orders bell. Like a journeyman boxer who's on the ropes and hanging on for dear life in the final round, the bell is a welcome sound. I've survived the Boxing Day madness and it's time to stagger up the hill and home. Somehow I manage to make it. The house is empty as my loved one is staying at her mum's in West London, so I sit in front of the TV and watch some old bloke pulling funny faces with his hand down the front of his trousers. I go to change channels and realise that the telly isn't even switched on. I thought he looked slightly familiar. It's time to call it a day.

Sunday 29th December 2013 – 4pm kick-off

Chelsea 2 Liverpool 1

We've hit the midway point of the season and I'll admit it, I'm flagging. It's the second away game in a few days and I'm worn out with it all. Maybe because it's Chelsea, one of my least favourite grounds in the league to visit, or maybe it's the drain on the finances for yet another London game. Whatever happened to all those Lancashire teams who were in the top flight a couple of years ago. Nice easy places to visit where you could be back in the pool of life, before the scousebirds had even had the chance to remove their curlers and paint those stupid Coco the clown eyebrows on, for a night on the town. Wigan, Burnley, Blackpool, Bolton Wanderers, Blackburn Rovers, easy games to get to. Gone forever to be replaced by teams in towns and cities in far off distant lands. Who would've thought teams like Cardiff and Swansea would one day grace the glittering international stage of the Premier League. Not me for sure, I still can't get my head around Crystal Palace being up. But anyway it's Chelsea today and I'm gonna have to drag myself down there. And hopefully witness something special against Mourinho's boys. I think I've just to get those old post Christmas blues out of my system.

We're aiming to get the 9.38 from Lime Street but Smigger has to wait on big Andy Nico for his match ticket. And with minutes to spare, he appears. Obviously Bootle, where he's just come from, must have its own microclimate, because oblivious to the biting cold of a late December morning, he appears in a pair of flip flops and t-shirt looking slightly dazed. Me and Smig look as though we are about to attempt to climb the north face of the Eiger, all woolly hats, boots and big coats, and he's strolling around like he's just coming down for breakfast by the pool in Tenerife. Scousers, eh, completely and utterly bonkers. We get the ticket and leg it onto the train with about a minute to spare. Once we get settled and have a cup of coffee, I take my hat off and it's only then that I realise that I haven't got a headache after all. Here's me thinking that I'm not 100% and all it was is that my hat was on too tight. What a div! I've got that many lines on my head now that I could probably screw my hat on. It's weird when you put something new on and you're not used to it. I remember when I first started wearing glasses, and I thought that my dick had grown. The first piss that I had with them on, I looked down and thought 'hello, big fella, what's this?' Had God finally granted me my first wish, and I was about to be whisked off to America to dominate the adult film industry? I would probably have to change my name to Hot Dodd or something. Then moving my eyes away from my new prized asset I noticed that my hands had grown as well. It was only when I lifted my glasses up slightly and peered down again that I realised that the game was up, and it had all been a teasing optical illusion. Oh well, not to worry.

We idly chat with our fellow Reds on the journey of our agreed dislike of Chelsea FC and all that it stands for. Chelsea were nobody until the Russian with the vacant expression and his sack full of dodgy roubles came calling. People who moan about the way that football has become morally bankrupt need look no further than the day Abramovich first walked down the Fulham Road. The madness of paying players in excess of £250,000 a week, now is almost considered normal and it shouldn't be. It's an outrage when you think that some players are getting paid millions to do nothing other than sit out a contract and Chelsea broke the mould. They outbid everyone for anyone and anyone for everyone. They were buying players that they didn't even use, just to stop other clubs buying them, and obviously paying them more than the going rate, which then opened the door for even more unscrupulous people to come in to join the English football circus. Even our own club was nearly purchased by the disgraced ex-Thai prime minister with his dubious millions. So the only way you could compete with the Chelsea's of this world is to sell your soul to any Tom, Dick or Hammed who comes calling. Now the league is full of nutty foreign owners, some alright, some absolutely stark raving mad.

Hull and Cardiff are this year's focal point for extreme egotistical madness and I'm sure they won't be the last. At least they're in the top flight as we speak, but anything can happen with schizophrenic owners who might just bail out at the drop of a hat. You've only got to look at the way that Portsmouth were shafted, now playing in the bottom division without a pot to piss in. Luckily at the moment, LFC seems to be running alright. Ok, it's a bit strange being owned by people from the US who hardly ever pay a visit and who know sweet FA about footy, but as you all know it has been worse in our not-too-distant past. So all in all, it's not the worst case scenario. But back to Chelsea, my third most hated club. You only have to compare the two neighbourhood environments to see how different the conflicting cultures of our respective clubs are. The postcodes of L4 and SW6 are about as far apart as you can get on the British mainland. One thing about Chelsea that has always done my head in and probably

Abramovich's as well is their phoney atmosphere. Going to the Bridge nowadays is almost akin to going to the Tory conference. Oh how they would love to emulate our famous Spion Kop. Since that spine tingling Champions League semi-final at Anfield, back in 2005, when the crowd basically scared the shit out of the southern softies, they've tried everything to copy us. The most embarrassing being the plastic flags for everyone fiasco. The London PR boys must've thought this'll show them, and it just looked like a load of kids welcoming the Queen on a Commonwealth visit to some outpost or at best, a communist rally. I remember when Torres escaped from the wild and ended up in the captivity of London. They welcomed him with a banner which had been copied directly from a Liverpool one and put on a blue background. What the soft cunts forgot to do was to take off the design of the Shankly Gates. Absolutely unforgivable. No class or originality whatsoever.

Anyway before we get to this ground, we need a few liveners and Earls Court is the chosen stopover for our pre-match aperitif. The Courtfield opposite the station is absolutely rammed with Redmen. Too rammed in fact to even get served, so we move along to The Prince of Tec which is busy but bearable. So we set up camp in there. John Macdonald and Steve Davis are in. If there's a bevvy, they're always in. There's so many faces that you see week in week out, and yet you don't even know half of their names. It's just "alright mate", "alright lad", "alright fella" all day long but we're all part of this big never-ending roadshow. We walk to the ground with Griffo and Poolio. It's fairly straight forward and I know it like the back of my hand, as me and a few mates lived in Earls Court square when I was a young tearaway in my late teens. Back in those days round here you were either Aussie or gay or both. We were neither but we had some of the best laughs down here. You could shag birds in this heaving metropolis from the most exotic of places. At home it would be Sandra from the cake shop or Sue from hairdressers but down here it was like BANG. Just like another world. You could be in love with a blondie from Sweden one minute and the next day you could be tasting the juices of a dusky brunette from Peru. Italians, Spanish, Brazilians, Filipinos. It was as though the whole world was here at your fingertips. For a lad of 18 it really was the University of Life. It's easy being streetwise on an insular estate back home but down here it was like switching from black and white to colour overnight. We had a ball but I imagine if you weren't working or lived in crappy accommodation it would probably be the loneliest place on earth.

The floodlights come into view and we have to go through the usual rigmarole of showing your ticket about five times to over-zealous stewards as they filter you towards the visitor's section. I'm at the front of about fifty of our fans as we are told to wait. Next minute the steward is getting all aggressive, shouting some nonsense in his mother tongue right into my face. He's pushing his hand into my chest. His eyes are bulging and the bloke next to me says "what's he on about?". He's just shouting "sack, sack, sack". It's a ridiculous situation. We've got a man who's been given far too much authority, who's getting physical with people who've paid a fortune to be here and to top it all off, he can't speak fuckin' English. A copper comes over to quell the commotion. I tell him that nobody can understand what on the earth the steward is saying. "Sack, sack" he says to the copper pointing at us. The copper has no idea what he's on about, and just says "It must be African or Nigerian for search. I think he wants to search you. Just open your arms and let him do what he's got to do." I'm fuming that I have to allow this twat manhandle me with no respect or manners. This is Chelsea

FC. I'm angry before I'm even in the ground. I'm gonna have to stop coming here. Every year it's the same pain in the fuckin' arse. And an expensive pain in the arse at that.

The game kicks off and we're up and at them straight from the word go. And within a minute Samuel Eto'o goes studs up right through Jordan Henderson. It's a sending off, no other option. But don't you for one second think that our old friend Howard Webb is going to send a Chelsea player off at Stamford Bridge in the first minute. Absolutely no chance. He doesn't even book him. I've watched it back loads of times and every pundit, commentator and journo without exception is unanimous. It's a red. These are big games and big decisions, and we are not getting any of them at the moment. While we're still seething by the injustice of it all, Skrtel only goes and scores from close range to send the Red hoards dancing down the aisles. It's a good start, but just like at City, we couldn't even hold out until half time. Chelsea bombarded us and Hazard curled the equaliser in after 17 minutes. And then just to rub salt into the wound, Samuel Eto'o scores what would turn out to be the winner on 34 minutes. I don't know what Mignolet was thinking of but he seemed to palm yet another mis-hit shot in slow motion into his own goal.

In the second half we were much better and Sakho hit the bar with a header but you just had the feeling that for the second time in a couple of days that the gods were against us. With seven minutes left, again Mr E'to brought Suarez down off the ball and in the area, and more importantly, right in front of Howard Webb. And to the amazement of everybody and to the disgust of Brendan Rodgers, you've guessed it, no penalty. That's two away games in three days against the two favourites for the title. Beaten both times 2-1 after leading early on. Both games marred by some terrible decisions against us. And both matches we played really well and matched them. But the bottom line is that we have no points to show for all that endeavour. I really hope that this doesn't knock us for six and we start to implode. Even though we've had a good go and probably should've beaten City, it's gonna be hard to motivate both the team and the fans for Hull at home on New Year's Day.

To go down from top to fifth in a week is a tough one to take, but this is when the manager, the players and us fans must stand up and be counted. This is not the time to listen to knobheads, moaning on radio phone-ins when they've never been to a match in their whole life. This is when we all find out what we're made of. At the moment I'm deflated. I'm tired and I could do with a break. A week in the sun would be nice, but I'm skint. Even a couple of footy free days in a cottage somewhere with a log fire would clear my head. Or maybe I could just go missing. You know like those people who just disappear for a month and then reappear claiming that they don't know where they've been or what they've been doing. I don't think that would somehow wash with my bird though. She'd just look at my innocent expression and say "Ok, man of mystery, you've had your laugh now, where the bleedin' hell have you been since a week last Monday?" and I'd say something like "Er dunno. I've lost me memory." Then she would cunningly lure me into her trap by saying "Oh you poor thing. I'll book a weekend in the Lakes for us in a fortnight. The weekend of the 11th / 12th Jan. Is that ok with you, darling?" And I'd foolishly reply "I can't, it's Stoke away that weekend" and she'd say "Ah ha, I've caught you. I thought you'd lost your memory. How come you can remember dates of football matches but not where you live?" Nah, it just wouldn't work.

There's more bad news. We know Fulham Broadway is closed but now the stadium announcer says that Earls Court station has a delay of ninety minutes, which is not good news at all. This means we have to walk to South Kensington tube, which is a bit of a hike. This is a seriously affluent area. We pass not one, not two, but three Aston Martins parked in a line just on the street. If one passes you at home, it's still a head turner, and you certainly wouldn't park it on the street, unless you had armed guards surrounding it. As I've said before, it's a different world down here at South West 6. There's a TV programme about the tosser community down here, which I refuse to watch. I think it's called The Only Way is Chelsea Shore or something, where they glamorise fake-ness, phoney-ness and general twatish-ness. And believe me there is no shortage of wannabe wealthy wankers willing to wave their wallets whilst wandering willy nilly through the well off, well-heeled Wodehouse world of one-upmanship. Oops sorry I just suffered a short attack of the W's there. Apologies all round.

I'm back on track now. I'm back on the tube and off at Euston. We stock up on provisions ready for the journey home and see Paul Randalls, the Cavos, and their little crew in The Bree Louise pub. Then we decide to go to The George for the final London pint. The train back is a masterclass in Liverpool football songs, compered, directed and performed on lead vocals by the wonderful, yet hopelessly drunk, Luke Daley. An equally inebriated John Mackin hears the call and appears from nowhere to assist on backing vocals. The ticket inspector, who has already handed out three final warnings, mysteriously disappears around Stafford. He's either changed trains or taken his own life. By the look on his face, I would say it was the latter.

Sunday 12th January 2014 – 4.10pm kick-off

Stoke City 3 Liverpool 5

The only redeeming feature about going to Stoke is that it's only about seventy miles away. I don't know anyone who actually looks forward to travelling there for our annual war of attrition. It's always a shit day out. Usually out-muscled and out-battled by a Tony Pulis team full of cloggers and journey men. I have no memory of sunny days and exciting matches played in front of fans in t-shirts with expectant smiles. No, a visit to Stoke, especially for recent Liverpool teams, is a grim experience. Cold, drab and painful to watch in a ground situated in a soul-less out of town retail park. I don't think I've ever bounced out of bed in the morning and thought, oh yes, it's Stoke City away, ooh I can't wait. No, it's one of those ones that you want to get out of the way. Get in, try and get the three points and get off. Mark Hughes has come in to take over and has tried to tame the infamous beast that Stoke City has become over the last few years. He's trying his best. The long throws have gone but some of the henchmen like Shawcross and Whelan remain. It's gonna be tough and Brendan got stung here last year, on his first visit as manager, in that gut wrenching Boxing Day defeat. It's time we stood up for ourselves.

The coach is full and the trains are dodgy on a Sunday, so I've decided to give the new motor a spin. The benefits are you can leave whenever you want, stop off when and where you want and even have food and a flask of hot coffee or whatever. The downside is, and this is a biggie, you can't drink (much) and that is a major minus for an awayday match experience. It was only the day before that I said I'd drive, so the others are all booked on the coach and train and as much as Bucko wants to come with us, he has to honour his booking. You can't be pulling out the day before. Big Phil would take a very dim view of that. So it's just me and Smig then. Up Scotty, past Castle Doom, along the Lancs and left into Southdene, Kirkby, home to a host of urban myths. Some true, some not so true, but a town that deservedly holds its place in Merseyside folklore. Smigger's up for it as always. His face is at the window like a kid waiting for the postman on his birthday. I reckon his missus, Sue, locks him in the basement every two weeks and then releases him just for away matches. We floor it down the M6 in no time at all. In fact, to be quite honest, I could've had another hour in bed.

We're in sight of the ground but we decide to hit a left and stop off at a watering hole away from the crowds. In keeping with our crusade to support local working men's clubs, we find ourselves in the cavernous and yet empty Jubilee WMC in Newcastle-under-Lyme. Strange name Newcastle-under-Lyme. I look up and can see no lyme, in fact I don't know what a lyme is. The more famous one is upon Tyne, so I understand that, a city on a river Tyne, but a town under lyme, sorry you've got me there. It should probably be renamed, Newcastle-the-one-by-Stoke, because if you are on holiday and somebody asked you where you were from, and you said Newcastle, they'd say "but you don't sound like a Geordie" and you'd say "no, Newcastle, the one by Stoke". It must've happened gazillions of times. Anyway the Jubilee WMC is empty apart from us and four elderly blokes who, all bar one, seem to be sporting rather large hooped earrings. It never fails to amuse me seeing pensioners with bits of jewellery dangling from their lobes. They're making a fashion statement which says I've been there lad. It's not a look that has ever caught on in and around the population of Merseyside, but here like many other places, it is seen as de rigeur. To me they just look like four old pirates hatching a plan to dig up the buried treasure. Oh well, each to their own. We move on to get a parking space by the ground, so we can make a quick getaway. An official looking young buck in his high-vis jacket points us to a spec, and then we are free to go and queue up at the only pub for miles.

It's freezing cold and there's about fifty people in a line outside The Harvester, waiting to gain access. Fuck that for a lark seems to be the general consensus. So we mooch around the back and in through the fire door with military precision. Inside are all the usual suspects, big Keith, Derry Dave, John Mackin, Mick Smith and you know, loads of people. I'm only allowed two pints so I'm in the unusual position of entering a football stadium in full control of all my faculties, preparing myself to endure the annual drab game in freezing temperatures. Well I didn't see this one coming. An eight goal thriller with the Redmen banging in five of them. We stand near the back with Hooto and Mono in front of us looking like they're gonna die of hyperthermia. Besides wearing the right sort of clothes, the other thing guaranteed to warm the cockles of a freezing football fan's heart is goals, and plenty of them. This season we seemed to have discovered the knack of scoring. A couple of years ago under Kenny, all we ever seemed to do was hit the woodwork. Some would say it was just down to bad luck, others would say it was crap marksmanship. Cissokho gets lucky after five minutes, when he just twats a random shot which is on its way to the M6 when it deflects off Shawcross and into the Stoke net. My god, lady luck has finally decided to smile on us. What kept you girl? Where have you been the last few years? Cissokho celebrates like he's done something amazing, like he's conjured up a little bit of magic but in all truth it was a bloody awful shot, from a player who's failed to impress since he's been here. But hey, I'm not complaining, in fact I'm buzzing. On 32 minutes, Suarez chases a lost cause when Marc Wilson and Shawcross get in a bit of a muddle and within in a flash Suarez is there to slot goal number two. And that should be that but with the way our defence has been since Carra jibbed it, anything can happen. And at places like Stoke, it usually does.

Before the travelling Kopites had had the chance to get through their full repertoire of celebratory battle songs, the Potters had pulled level with two goals in the last six minutes of the half. Somebody called Peter Crouch powered a header past Mignolet and then right on the whistle another bloke by the name of Charlie Adams blasts one in from twenty yards out. Now where have we heard their names before? All the hard work and early dominance undone yet again by crap defending. That's seven out of the last eight games that we've conceded two or more away from home. Downstairs at the break the fans are annoyed. The general consensus is that things could get a lot worse unless Brendan can galvanise the troops, and get them to focus more on what they're supposed to be doing. Within six minutes of the restart we're back in the lead. Sterling blocks a clearance and runs into the box from the half way line. Wilson whose clearance it was tries to make amends, but brings young Raheem down for a bit of a soft penalty. Gerrard who is back after injury and playing in a deeper role slots the spot kick to make it 3-2 on his 650th Liverpool appearance. Coutinho is then replaced by Daniel Sturridge, who is another one who is back after a six week lay-off. Almost immediately he goes on a tricky run, then gives a peach of a pass to Suarez, who buries it into the corner. That will do nicely. The gloom of the Staffordshire cold and incessant rain seems to lift for a short while. That is until Mignolet lets a weak under-hit shot from that bluenose buffoon John Walters squirm under him to make it 4-3. Fuckin' 'ell, this team of ours never makes it easy for themselves.

It's not the first howler from our new goalie but in all fairness, he's been great in a lot of games this season, so I'm not going to have a go, but we can't be having too many more of these because Luis can't keep bailing the defence out every week. We have a few close shaves but Sturridge wraps it up with a really good finish at the back post, after Suarez picks him out. Daniel is visibly delighted to have hit the winner and so are we. I'm glad we never came by train now because it is absolutely pissing down and we would have had to negotiate buses out of this retail park hell hole and find the station, whereas we can just shoot off in the car and bomb it back to the pool of life in just over an hour. Hot Lips is on the starting blocks back at Dodd Towers. She is primed and ready to go. The plan is that I drop the car and me and Smig get in her car, and she drops us off at the pub of our choice in town where we can meet hush Hoskins, aka Captain Bucko, the noisiest man in the universe. The switch is completed like an American undercover cop show. Almost seamless. You might think it sounds a bit selfish, me being out all day and then just jumping from one car to another, like someone doing something important, but you have to understand that matchday is my day. There are plenty of other days where the imprint of the long suffering Hot Lips will leave its mark. She knows how happy this 'following the Reds' thing makes me feel. But there will be times when she is the director of the show we call life. It's been another successful mission.

Sunday 2nd February 2014 – 1.30pm kick-off

West Bromwich Albion 1
Liverpool 1

I've been walking around town for the last few days looking the like the cat who'd got the cream. It's amazing what a derby win can do for your self-esteem. Since the 4-0 hammering of those lovable, shy, retiring bluenoses on Tuesday night, I've spent most of my time since trying to seek them out and make their pathetic little lives even more unbearable than usual. Most have gone underground, failing to show for work, not answering phones etc., but fear not readers, your pain in the arse author has done his duty. I've found them hiding in garden sheds, the trauma wings in hospitals, living rough down by the river, even walking around town with false beards and unnecessary headgear to try and evade the attentions of their more cultured, civilised, knowledgeable Red neighbours. The bitter ones have taken it badly. They've talked this game up for weeks as the one when they finally break the Anfield hoodoo voodoo. Fourteen years since they last tasted victory on this hallowed turf and all the positivity of Martinez was to be crushed underfoot, long before half time. Even the usual animosity, venom and grudge bearing resentment seemed to be absent from the primitive philistines in the away section of the Anfield Road. Demolition Derby read the headlines Outclassed said another. This was probably the most one-sided thrashing in a derby for years. And the boys in blue knew it.

Whilst they're still in the recovery position, we the Mighty Redmen march on to West Bromwich Albion, home of the boing boing Baggies. We got stuffed here last year on Brendan's first game in charge, but eighteen months on we are a more settled and focused type of team. The day starts with a bit of a hiccup as Ally commits the unforgivable sin of over sleeping and missing the train. Me, Parso and Smigger leave Lime Street on the 9.38, and change at Stafford and then again at Wolverhampton and a quick final change at Smethwick Galton Bridge. Then a two minute hop to the Hawthorns, which leaves us just under two hours to have a drink in the Royal Oak on Handsworth Road.

I ring Tommy O'Hagan to see how he's getting on with the old big C. It's soul destroying as he's on the other end of the line but he can't speak. He's just making a croaky sound. About half an hour later his daughter Andrea phones to say it's now spread to his throat and his voice has gone. He's written her a message to relay to us. Basically saying he's not well, but for us to have a good day and bring the three points home. God bless the King of the Press-Ups. The peace is disturbed when a tetchy Bucko arrives wearing a cowpat on his head. You know the type; kind or roaring twenties, New York prohibition style of hat, that Supergran used to wear. He's only been here a couple of minutes and he's upset the apple cart already. He's ranting on about everything from beer to tickets to which way the wind is blowing. Someone's obviously upset him. And it's us poor three souls who are bearing the brunt of his frustration. It's out of character but it still drags the mood of the pre-match bevvy down a notch. As we get into the ground Bucko disappears up the stairs like one of those twisters you see in the States that disturb everything in their path. We get up to the back row with Smigger's mate Suki, who's Indian and from around Handsworth. He's known him for about thirty years. He's offering to take us for a bevvy after the game, to the pubs where he goes. It's gonna be a bit weird as although we're all men of the world, and I've been to Goa on a number of occasions, I don't think any of us, other than Smigger have knocked around with British Asians in their community before. Should be interesting and Parso's always up for a bit of peace, love and harmony. He buzzes off a bit of that 'hands across the cultural divide' stuff. On the other hand, we all agree that it's a blessing that Danny Giles isn't on board today. He would undoubtedly cause a diplomatic incident by saying something really outrageous in his quest for the perfect comedy one-liner.

Now at this point a few of you who know my good self might be saying, "Hang on a mo. Isn't Jegsy's bird of the Asian persuasion?" and I'd have to concede and say "Yes. Hot Lips is of Indian stock. But we hardly live on the curry mile, so we never come into contact with your run of the mill Asian geezers. Wirral is, whether you like it or not, as white as anywhere on the British mainland. She is quite proud to call herself 'the only brown in the village'. Anyway, we'll see what happens after the game.

The first half was nothing special. They had a few chances and we had a couple, but this was a world away from the intensity of the Everton game in midweek. Sturridge scored in his fifth game on the trot, to make it 1-0 but it was far from convincing from the Reds. We go down at half time and I bump into my old mate Zug (Dave Burrows) who's with his daughter Steph. He's been living in Reading for about twenty five years now but was my bezzy mate at primary school about two centuries ago. It's good to see the old spunker, even if he has lost his accent. We arrange to meet in the Oak after the game. The second half was bitterly disappointing, the main talking point being West Brom's equaliser which was as bad a goal as you'll ever see. Kolo Toure, what on earth were you thinking of. With absolutely no pressure and plenty of options, he decides to play a perfect pass across his own box to ex-Evertonian Victor Anichebe who calmly slots past Mignolet. It was a terrible mistake and one that has cost us two points when really we should be twatting teams like West Brom. You think to yourself what's the point of walloping Everton in midweek and then coming here and struggling. Make no mistake, it was Toure's fault but overall we weren't really at the races today. It always seems to happen after we've played really well. Successful teams have to be fired up, week after week after week. We're still in the mix though, so we have to get our heads sorted and be ready for the Arsenal next weekend. And if those heads drop there will be no sexy matches against Europe's elite in the Champions League next year. It'll be just endless treks to nowheres-ville in the Europa Poo Pants League. Perish the thought.

We're back at that Royal Oak and it's absolutely full to the brim again. The Baggies in there are obviously quite pleased with a point and are friendly with it. The Injuns show up and Suki wants to take us to a boozer by Perry Barr dog track, called the Seventh Trap or something. Me, Parso, Smig and a more mellow hush Hoskins (Bucko) squash into his car, while Zug and daughter get a cab. We are treated with the finest hospitality. Huge plates of spicy barbecue chicken pieces come over with mint yoghurt dips and naan bread. Proper Indian gear for the Redmen. And it's all on the house, which is always a bonus. You don't get this in the King Harry on match days. There's even a Liverpool Istanbul scarf behind the bar and a picture of King Kenny keeping watch. The beer is flowing and the opening bars of You'll Never Walk Alone drift from the jukey in the corner. That's it. We're up. We have a communal sing song which stretches from Help by some Liverpool band to The Beat, The Specials, Madness and some superb air trumpeting on Geno by Dexy's Midnight Runners. It's a great spontaneous and unexpected night. Ritchie and them have been back in the Pool of Life for hours. But we're still in Brum having a whale of a time. I nip outside for a quick smoke and end up getting stoned with the only Rasta in the place. And you'll never guess who he used to play the drums for? Only Steel Pulse, one of my fave reggae bands of all time who did the classic album Handsworth Revolution. My day is complete. I send texts to anyone and everyone I know who is connected with music to share my joy. Maybe I'm going a little OTT and maybe it's just the old cannabis / lager cocktail that is the catalyst for my wide-eyed juvenile joy but who gives a fuck. I'm happy. My travelling companions are less ecstatic when I tell them. "Who?", "Never heard of 'em", "What did they sing then?" I have vague recollections of Parso giving me half a nod of recognition, but from the others, it's a big no.

We somehow manage to get a minibus to New Street station and negotiate a train to Crewe, while Bucko heads back down to Londinium and Zug to Reading. As we fall off the rattler at Lime Street, Parso who's had trouble staying awake on the last leg of this epic day bids us farewell. Me and Smig have one last bevvy in Ally's pub to tell him what he's been missing. It's been a great away day and Ally's gutted he missed it. Then just as he asks how much he owes for the train ticket, my befuddled marinated brain has a cunning plan. "You know those train tickets you've got in your pocket Smig. Well I hope you realise that we haven't had them checked all day. Do you reckon if we give them to Ally to take back tomorrow we'll get a refund?", "Don't know lad, it's worth a go." So we say to Ally as punishment for oversleeping your mission tomorrow is to present yourself at the ticket office and plead insanity. Two days later after a ten pound deduction, for administrative costs, we collect £78 back off said tickets. And everyone is happy. The next morning Hot Lips tells me that I was that pissed when I got in that I was convinced that I had been getting stoned with Kolo Toure and he plays the drums in a reggae band…. Mmmm that probably explains that pass to Anichebe. Somebody needs to tell Brendan Rodgers before the papers find out.

Wednesday 12th February 2014 – 8pm kick-off

Fulham 2 Liverpool 3

I'd been looking forward to this one for a while. We'd booked the Alhambra Hotel off Euston Road weeks ago and bought our train tickets well in advance, so we had peace of mind. But there was a problem. Danny's text was the first to arrive, as usual. 'Bad news. Game at Fulham in doubt. Tube strike.' If ever there was a person who revelled at other people's misfortune, it is this man. Even when I had a cheeky week away on the international break, a text came in. 'Air traffic controllers strike in France. No flights allowed. That includes Tunisia.' He must just sit there praying for ash clouds or hurricanes or hijackings, scouring the internet for things that could go wrong because he's not going. Then he rings with that firm, in-the-know voice that loves to break the bad news. 'I'm just saying like…' but you know he's buzzing. Well I'm afraid this time he could be right. The match is in serious doubt and you can't cancel the hotel less than 24 hours before your stay. The unions are in talks and the announcement is to be made after 3pm the day prior to the match. Luckily the strike was called off and the game was to go ahead. The relief was massive and the panic over.

The previous weekend was an absolute belter. My nephew Joey was soon to be going back to Germany and wanted to come up to Anfield for the Arsenal game. I managed to snaffle him a ticket but warned him not to expect anything like the Tottenham result. But the performance in that first half last week ranked as one of the greatest the Kop has ever witnessed. To be 4-0 up in less than twenty minutes, against the top of the table team and missing a sitter and hitting the post, was phenomenal, jaw-dropping stuff.

Today our mission is to go down to Craven Cottage against the bottom club and carry on where we left off. Oh, if only life was just that easy. Me and Smig are joined in Lime Street by last minute addition Dave Kirby, who must've passed a very late fitness test and been deemed fit to travel by his wife. We get into Euston and are met by another Kirkby lad, Gary, who's working down in Dartford. The odds are stacked against me. That's three Kirkby commandos and the just the one from 'the other side'. It's got all the makings of a great away day. But hang on a mo, who's this? Yep, it's none other than Captain Bucko, Lord of Lords, aka The Reverend Babycakes (don't ask). Yes, he's here. You didn't think for one minute I would alight the train in London without Bootle's finest welcoming me to the great metropolis. Not on your nelly. It's probably written on the small print on my train ticket – 'you will be met by The Man when you arrive at your destination'.

Now the only down side to this, and it's only a very small downside, is that Bucko always has a plan, an itinerary. Whether you like it or not, he has decided where you are going and what you will be doing. Now we are four well-travelled free-thinking adult males who may have made the odd important decision along life's rocky road, maybe have even held an opinion or two, if pushed, but all that counts for nothing when the Captain is your unofficial tour guide. Every suggestion is dismissed, as if it were the worst idea ever. "Nah, it's shite there. Listen to me. Follow your Uncle Bucko and you won't

Bucko, me and Dave on the way to
the World Frowning Championships

go far wrong. Right we're going here, then there, then there, then there…" and the list goes on. No debate. No ifs. No buts. It always happens, every time. And for the life of me I cannot remember ever having a vote on him being Expedition Leader or Commander In Chief, as he likes to be known. You've got to love him though. He's a complete one-off. You get to the pub and there's always an assortment of other bewildered people there who he has already captured in his charismatic web of nuttiness. But this time we have a genuine excuse. We have bags and we have to check in our hotel by Kings Cross. It's like we're on a school trip and we've given the teacher the slip. We even have a sneaky pint on the way to meet him in The Friend. It's only a quick one in somewhere called McGlynn's or O'Glynn's or something, but he's on the phone and he's not best pleased. This is seen as a slur on his leadership qualities. We drink up and race to Russell Square to appease the 'Not So Chosen One'. Mercer arrives with the biggest rucksack in history on his back. You could fit a fridge freezer in there and still have space for a wardrobe. Trekking in the Himalayas for three months, you might think. "No, I'm just staying at me dads in Dover for a couple of days." "Blimey, people take less to Oz when they're emigrating."

We get the tube to Putney Bridge and cross said bridge to the other side of the Thames to meet Mercer's dad who's parked over there. Within minutes we find ourselves in a pub called The Coat & Badge, which is not the greatest name for a boozer, if the truth be known, but it serves its purpose. Chris, from Brighton is in there with a little crew, sorry I meant to say Chris from Kirkdale, who lives in Brighton, is there with his mates. He's another one who's completely barmy. He could walk up and just spontaneously human combust in front of you and someone would just say "Oh, it's only Chris havin' a laugh". Yet another character who gives going to the match that edginess and potential for the unexpected. About as far removed from a forgettable family friendly Fulham football fan as you can get. Who says there's not enough 'f words' in this book. We head back down to the river and walk through a pub called The Yacht, to another which I think was called The Ship. It's here where news comes through that City v Sunderland and Everton v Palace have both been called off due to seriously bad weather. It's a bit cold here on the old banks of the Thames but nothing like what it seems up north. We march back over the bridge and up to the ground for the start of the match.

You always hope that we don't falter in games like this after such a scintillating win over Arsenal. West Brom being a case in point after the derby match. But what do we do? We get caught sleeping straight from the off. Fulham are all over us in the first five minutes and could've scored twice. Then on eight minutes Kolo Toure carries on his comedy routine by inexplicably slicing the ball into his own net while under no pressure at all. If you thought his pass to Anichebe at the Hawthorns ten days ago was bad, this was even worse. Our forward play may be world class this season but some of our defending has been woeful. Surely a club of our size shouldn't have to panic every time there's a corner conceded or a routine set piece to defend, but the reality is we have to score probably three or four to make sure we win. Entertaining, yes. But avoidable, also yes. It needs sorting and sorting quick style.

Fulham continue to press and make chances. And Liverpool continue to allow them. We needed inspiration and as half time loomed it was Steven Gerrard, as usual, who provided that spark. Four minutes before the break he pounced on a mistake by the halfway line and produced the pass of the season. With the outside of his boot he curled a defence splitting ball into the path of the prolific Daniel Sturridge who slotted it past Maarten Stekelenburg in the Fulham goal to make it 1-1 half time. The second half starts and predictably the Reds really go for it. Brendan's team talk looks like it may have just worked. Suarez hits a post and we are all over them. But as happened many times this season, just when you think we are going to nail them, our defence opens the door to the gift shop again. This time Skrtel gets himself in a tangle and slices it to Richards who says thank you very much and taps it in at the far post. It's end to end stuff, what commentators call 'great for the neutrals'. But I've got to be honest, I don't know any neutrals who actually go to matches. This is edge of the seat stuff. On seventy two minutes Coutinho gets us level after bending one in, after a run across the box. The away following is rocking. The support that Liverpool get at all their matches on their travels is absolutely outstanding. It's a cold Wednesday night in south west London. Miles from home and our end is packed in like sardines. Add to that we've got a cup game down here in only four days at Arsenal and there will be even more down here for that, but as the great man Shankly once said "This is our bread and butter. This is the one we want to win more than anything." The Emirates on Sunday may well be glamorous but this is far, far more important. We are playing here for the long term future of this club, whether it's Champions League qualification or the holy grail of winning this elusive fucking Premier League, the modern day league that always seem too far over the other side of the mountain and out of sight of us believers, year after year.

Anyway time is running out. The fans are urging the boys home over the finish line, and then it happens. Sturridge, who's been a revelation this season, gets upended in the box in the last minute. Oh please God, this is proper pressure. This is a big big penalty. It's a massive moment in the season. Three thousand secret turtle heads appear then quickly disappear, as Stevie steps up and absolutely twats it high into the net. Cue utter mayhem. Big Vinny Ooo-ar has got me in a headlock. Bucko looks like he's on a trampoline. There's red smoke bombs going off. This is as important a win as any this season. The whistle goes and I'm not ashamed to say "I believe".

As we stream out of the ground, we are still singing and dancing as we go past that park on the way to the tube. We toast the boys in Red at a pub called The Lark, where the wide-eyed joyous devotees gather to celebrate another famous victory. It's here where I foolishly get drawn into an argument with some pompous Anglo-Indian businessman, who lives in the good ol' USA. Sacramento to be exact. He starts off by claiming to be Liverpool's No. 1 fan, which obviously he isn't because his last match was Alaves in 2001. He proceeds to tell us that Liverpool as a soccer club need to think about re-branding. What?? Number 1, I hate the word soccer. It always seems to be used by non-football people when they are trying to patronise people who follow the world game. Number 2, now as much as the word soccer makes my toes curl, buttocks clench and brow furrow, the word 'brand' is another American phrase which has crept into the English league in the last few years. This constant marketing of anything and everything we hold dear, this Americanisation of the globe where everything must have a dollar sign on it, I absolutely hate it with a vengeance. Ian Ayre would probably take exception by saying "Hey we gotta move with the times dude. It's all about sponsorship." Well if that means selling our soul to the ridiculously named Dunkin' fuckin' Donuts to gain credibility, I'm afraid I don't get it. What next? Are we gonna hold a press conference where we announce, with a straight face, that we'd like to welcome Willie's Wanky Waffles as our new partner, or Chuck's Chunky Chicken titbits, because they pay more. For fuck's sake let's get some perspective. We can't just go on prostituting this club of ours to the highest bidder of the most stupidly named dollar rich company. Anyway I'm trying to deal with this prick from Sacramento when I ask him what type of re-branding he has in mind. "Maybe calling ourselves Liverpool Red Sox", I sarcastically say. "It's a possibility" he says. By now I must confess that I am subconsciously planning his departure from the human race. He continues with that annoying management speak, talking about Suarez as a commodity. I'm thinking of more basic things, like where do we go to hide the body. In the end, after telling him to go back to where he came from and to immediately stop supporting Liverpool Football Club, because people like him are not welcome, I have to turn my back on him. The thought of life imprisonment became just a little bit too much of an obstacle. But this is a big wake-up call for everyone, because this is the new type of fan we are attracting nowadays. They have to be stopped for the common good of this unique club of ours.

We get the tube to Soho but I'm still miffed about the Anglo-Indian American tosser in the pub. We've just had a great last minute win away from home and I should be buzzing but I'm pissed off that people like that are amongst our ranks. Our next stop is Club 47 on Greek Street, where the big jolly bouncer actually beckons us in, and wants to try out his comedy routine on us. Happy sociable doormen, hey, whatever next? We grab some seats and watch the bright young things of London make some shapes. Next minute an incoherent Scottish bloke plonks himself down next to me with a bottle of expensive champagne, in a bucket with six glasses. He's even got a strange vase type thing filled with ice and topped with strawberries and raspberries. Don't ask me, I haven't got a clue either. The barmaid appears and pours the champers so I say "where's your mates?" He just nods at the champagne and nods at me. Well the Kirkby three are loving this. They are convinced that our new mate is gay and that he wants to interfere with ME. I'm trying to play the situation down saying he's probably just lonely, but they're not having any of it. I'm almost acting like his defence lawyer pleading his case. I put it to the prosecution that why would the innocent inebriated jock be interested in cosying up to probably the most ineligible weather-beaten, heterosexual specimen on the premises. I ask the imaginary jury to cast their eyes around the room to the hordes of athletic looking nubile males and ask why me? If we lined up say a hundred of the blokes in here for some sort of 'Mr Wow Factor' or the 'Who Would You Like to See Naked?' contest, I'd probably be hovering around the 97th mark, with only my travelling companions battling it out for the final three places. But still the pissed Kirkby three carry on their persecution of the Wirral one. I sum up for the jury in a couple of sentences, the drunken Scotsman is probably just a champagne socialist who has come into a couple of bob, either working in the city or getting lucky in a casino. As for my good self it has to be said that my bottom has been one-way traffic for the whole of its lifetime. And no animal, vegetable or mineral has breached its defences. So I conclude that it is case dismissed with not guilty verdicts all around. We call it a night and get into an illegal taxi driven by a big mama with a deep African voice. "Feefteen pounz to Keengs Cross" answered by "Fuck off, ten quid, where's your licence? You're not even a proper taxi." Job done, ten pounds it is then. After a 4am visit to McDonalds for an array of artery clogging junk food, we retire for the evening.

I'm awoken from my deep slumber by Smigger the insomniac, who tells me Dave and Gary are waiting outside for us. Not even time for a shower to combat the inevitable hangover. Just a quick wash, brush teeth and check out. We're on the 11.07 and there's a backlog at Euston, so we have to be on the ball to get a seat. All the bad weather last night means there's been cancellations, so the station is rammed. Sully, Dicko and Tony Hall and their band of merry men are outside and they reckon we'll be lucky to get home this afternoon. On the big station concourse there's John Mac, Jimmy Blundell and co, and they reckon the best bet is to just guess what platform the Liverpool train will come in on and get on as quick as poss. So there we are, about fifteen hungover Redmen standing on a random empty platform, when you'll never in a million years guess who just walks casually behind us on his own, pulling a little travel case on wheels. Only Alex fuckin' Ferguson. Well knock me down with a feather. I always wondered what I'd say to him if I met him. I think he took us as much by surprise as we did him.

"Fuckin' 'ell it's Taggart."

"Hey bacon face. How's your chosen one getting on?"

"Thought Howard Webb would be carrying your case."

"Have you still got the FA in your back pocket?"

But it was all over in about twenty surreal seconds, as a railway guard rescued him and put him in a secure part of what turned out to be the Manchester train. The fifteen or so hungover Scousers looked stunned.

"Wow. How weird was that?"

And on a scale of weirdness that would have to be nine and a half out of ten. Two things though. The first is, I thought he got off fairly lightly, because although there was a few verbals and the odd bit of swearing, nobody approached him within ten yards and no one threatened him. The other thing was that I always imagined him to travel with a bit of an entourage or be driven everywhere by chauffeur but there he was, with no minder, no wife, no business people or hangers on. Just plain old whisky face, on his own travelling back to his underground lair. Well I must admit I didn't expect that. It's not our platform so we head back up to the crowds on the main concourse.

Just when you thought life couldn't get any stranger, everybody's looking up at the boards for details of departures when somebody shouts "I don't believe this. What are you doing here?" One of the lads has spotted Gary Neville with a couple of mates standing right behind us. I'm thinking what's going on here. It's like all the baddies from your dreams have decided to appear in reality on a main line station on a Thursday morning. I can't get my pickled head round it. Normally I'm quite sharp and fairly quick witted but I can barely focus, never mind say anything amusing to the man who openly hates my beloved team. He looks a bit nervous, which is to be expected, but give him his due, he stands his ground and just wants to talk footy. To think of all the times I've laid in bed at night after another soul destroying defeat at Old Trafford wondering what terrible things I would do if ever I met Gary Neville in the flesh and what do I do when it really happens? I just stand there looking like I've been injected with horse tranquiliser. All heavy eyelids with mouth hanging open. Again no one is nailing him with a really funny put down. I somehow feel like I've let the side down. The platform number is announced and there's a huge stampede as all reserved seats are null and void. There's not even a basic buffet. It's just pack 'em on and get 'em home.

We sit by Dave Kirby mates, Mick Foley and Phil Santy, who I know through being a mate of Steve Riley who is one of the city centre's legendary characters. Big Kev who is the chef at The Sandon is with them as well. We finally arrive in Liverpool and everybody has important things to do. Dave has to be back in town in a couple of hours for something on Radio Merseyside. Smigger has to check on his dad, etc. But me? I'm gonna do what I always do after a mad night away. I'm going straight to bed to have a few hours before Hot Lips gets in. Obviously in my dreams I will probably be kung fu-ing the dastardly Mr Neville all around Euston station, but then maybe not. I may finally have grown up.

Saturday 1st March 2014 – 5.30pm kick-off

Southampton 0 Liverpool 3

Today's match is going to be yet another overnight stopover which must be some sort of a record for us. Let's hope at the end of the season we can get rid of a few southern teams and see a couple of ones from the North or the Midlands get promoted. One team that won't be going down is Southampton. They've been a breath of fresh air this season and today is one of those matches that could go either way. We're going by car today with Pooley and Griff who hail from the leafy suburbs of Rainhill. They are mere boys compared to me and Smig. We've got a good twenty years on them and it should be a big step up in class for them to listen to me moaning for the next thirty hours. The two veterans wait for the two apprentices outside St George's Hall at the unsightly hour of 8am. A brand new Audi screeches up driven by Poolio and I have to say I'm impressed. Normally I would say "I didn't know the market for crack cocaine was so buoyant in Rainhill?" but these ain't no hustlers. These is good boys, both in responsible well paid jobs and most important of all, really good company. We set off on the long trek listening to the hilarious CD 'The Yamaha Years' by John Shuttleworth. It's a proper sing-a-long of absolute nonsense and everyone's buzzing.

We're just starting to feel how wonderful life is when THUD!!. The first text comes in just after nine. Tommy O'Hagan the legend has passed away this morning. It feels as if we've just skidded off the motorway and plunged into a river. The music is turned off immediately. For the next three hours or so the phone doesn't stop. Everybody loved Tommy. He was like our tribal elder, one of the last old school socialists. He may have been 74 but he still went to all the European aways and partied like a 25 year old. Although famous for his fifty press ups in the pub after the game, he could still manage to shift a considerable amount of ale before leading the troops into numerous renditions of Kop choir classics. There's loads of great stories about Tommy's exploits and adventures but my favourite one is when he left us in Ned Kelly's in town to get the last train home to Wigan. Obviously he'd had a few to drink and somehow ended up on a train in a deep sleep. The train comes to a halt and he's at Glasgow Central. So he gets off and thinks 'well I can't phone home at this time of night so I'll just hang around and get the first one back in the morning'. So after missing his stop by about 200 miles he bunks back on the first train going south the next day. He gets settled and drifts off again into a deep sleep and is awoken by a jolt as the train pulls into Birmingham New Street station, another hundred miles south of where he needed to get off. With rail replacements and a limited Sunday service he finally arrives back at the marital home mid-afternoon to be greeted by a concerned Margaret.

"Where the hell have you been?"

"I've been to the match."

"The match finished 24 hours ago."

"Yeah I know, but I got a bit lost on the way home."

People pay comedy script writers fortunes for stories like that. Tommy played the lead role in his own real life adventure. He was the storyline. A genuine Liverpool legend who will be sadly missed by all those match-heads who were lucky enough to share his company. The general theme coming from all the texts I'm receiving is that we have to win today for Tommy. I know that sounds a bit shallow but that's what he'd have wanted.

We check into the Premier Inn and get ourselves sorted. We've made good time so we can afford to have a decent bevvy before the 5.30pm kick-off. Looks like some of our fellow Redmen are already off to a flyer as I bump into a wide-eyed Scouser coming out of the toilets oblivious to the Columbian marching powder all over his face and down the front of his black t-shirt. Things could get a little crazy as the day wears on. Griffo has a weird obsession with wanting to get taxis everywhere, even when we're right in the city centre and we can see the pub in the distance. Which inevitably means the driver will take us on a tour of Southampton's one way system and then charge us accordingly. To put it in context, a Stoke City player could take a long throw from where we started and probably land it on the head of the bar man in the Yates Wine Lodge. Anyway we're in there and it's full of Liverpool but not many of the usual suspects, more of the football tourist, out-of-towner fraternity. I'm not knocking them. We all have the same goal, to see the Reds win. It's just that I don't know many of them, so we go off in search of a real pub, an independent non-chain type of establishment. We find an absolute gem, The Red Lion. It's the oldest pub in town and was built in the late 15th or early 16th century and is a Grade II listed building. Henry V used to bevvy in here with his mates before going over to Agincourt in 1415 to batter the French. There's even a part of it that was used as a late medieval courtroom which still remains to this day. I know I'm sounding a bit like a crusty old tour guide here getting all hysterically historical but places like this are brill. I mean let's face facts, you don't get this in your Popworld or your Slug & Friggin' Lettuce.

We move on to the less spectacular Southampton British Legion for a couple of rounds of extremely cheap drinks under the watchful eye of our new mate Steve. Steve is one of those helpful people who, without asking, has decided that we need his assistance and running commentary all the way to our turnstiles at the stadium. He tells us that that he has family on the Leasowe Estate in Wallasey and how he's drank in the notorious Oyster Catcher pub there. We shake hands and bid him farewell with over the top exaggerated smiles and thank you's. We even arrange to meet him after the match. In the queue I say "We're not seriously gonna meet him are we?" "Are we fuck" comes the not unexpected reply. Phew! Thank God for that.

We get into the ground and the atmosphere is really good. It's probably the late kick-off time that makes it a bit noisier because of the extra couple of hours to lubricate the vocal chords. Southampton are no mugs, so to get anything from here today the Redmen will need to be at their very best. Suarez as always was pivotal to everything Liverpool did on the break, and it was he who broke the deadlock on 16 minutes. He pounced on a ricochet off the unlucky Fonte and slotted it within a blink of the eye. Big celebrations all around. The crowd are beginning to sense this could be a special season after so long in the wilderness. Mignolet gets back into my good books with a stunning one-handed save to thwart the excellent Jay Rodriguez. If that would have gone in I reckon the whole game would've changed. We even survive an Adam Lallana shot hitting the post but after that we take complete control.

Downstairs at half time I'm trying to organise a mass press-up in memory of the much loved Tommy but alcohol is confusing matters. So I just drop to the floor and attempt my own tribute which is immediately sabotaged by some spoiler who decides to sit on my back leaving me face down on the beer soaked floor. Sorry Tommy, but you know what it's like amongst this travelling asylum. I did try. Suarez is trying, in fact he's tormenting the poor old Saints. He latches onto a pass by Gerrard around the hour mark and picks a perfect pass to Sterling who gleefully scores to give us that two goal cushion. Southampton are gutted because they've had a right good go but we've been more clinical. We used to be like that under Kenny. Always so close yet so far, always another hard luck story. I'm a great believer in 'you make your own luck'. To round off an almost perfect away performance Luis gets brought down in the box and Stevie blasts home the penalty. You can sense the buzz. The team come over to applaud the fans. The manager is beaming. This is a big, big win. People have to take us seriously now and for the first time this season the fans finally sing "And now you're gonna believe us. We're gonna win the league." It feels weird after all the shit we've had to put up with over the recent past with people like Hicks and Gillett and not being in Europe and players snubbing transfers here to go to lesser clubs. Well they can all fuck right off, because as we leave the ground I feel convinced that the Mighty Reds are coming up the hill. The summit is in sight and the Redmen are marching. This calls for a pint.

The four of us who are staying meet up and walk aimlessly around looking for a watering hole. After what seems like ages we finally roll up a boozer with a bit of a mouthful of a name. The Admiral Sir Lucius Curtis pub. We've no idea who he was but to have a place this size named after you, you would have to be quite important. He was probably one of Southampton's top boys back in the day. It's a huge pub and it's packed to the rafters with match going locals. As usual we try to keep a low profile but again, as always happens, all that goes out of the window after a few bevvies. We go to another couple of places nearby but they're all three deep at the bar and there's queues and bouncers to deal with. Griffo, who I mentioned earlier, loves to get taxis, is hailing them here, there and everywhere. Again it's another 'around the block' job when we could've cartwheeled there. Somehow we find ourselves back in The Red Lion but by now the livers are creaking under the pressure. Somebody has the bright idea to go back to the British Legion. "Hey letsh shee if Shteve's shtill in there?" The Steve who we stood up after the game has now taken on drunken significance. "Yesh, letsh shee Shteve." So we stagger round to the half empty crap British Legion with its pensioners and 'care in the community's jousting for supremacy on its Phoenix Nights dancefloor. "Where's Shteve?" we say to the barmaid. "Oh he left about three hours ago love". "OK, tell him hish besht matesh from Liverpool had come to shee him". We then sat down and watched all the weird and wonderful creatures dance out of time to the usual guff that gets played in these places. Another quick one in a Wetherspoons as the last orders bell goes. Dave Griff has a bit of a nark with a local over the merits of Steven Gerrard but the veteran two of the four manage to diffuse any impending affray that loomed. We get back to the hotel courtesy of another hundred yard taxi ride hailed by, yes you've guessed it, 'the boy who couldn't walk'.

I come out of my near coma state and go down to the breakfast room in search of the others. Smigger has had his over an hour ago. The apprentices are just starting to tuck in. I ask them what's the score. Obviously none of them have paid for their £8.99 all you want banquet. All I have to do is wait until the defence opens up, then ghost in and get a plate and look confident. Even though I've only been awake five minutes I manage to complete the blag with the minimum of fuss. I'm so glad I don't have to drive home. That task is left for

Pooley. Just give him his water and pop the John Shuttleworth CD on and we'll be home in no time. I must admit I'm not feeling 100%. I think my get up and go, got up and went before I even woke up this morning. I take comfort in the knowledge that I will never feel as bad as coming home from Swansea where it felt like we were on an off road jeep safari for five hours. This is at least in a straight line home. We haven't got a game for two weeks so I'm gonna go away with me loved one and get over this trip, recharge me batteries, do a bit of writing and just chill. When I get back there'll be the funeral, Parso's 50th and the most watched match in world football, so I think I'll just put the brakes on for a week. 2nd in the League…get in there!

Sunday 16th March 2014 – 1.30pm kick-off

Manchester United 0 Liverpool 3

There are few pleasures in life that beat the feeling of seeing the Mighty Reds from Anfield destroying their arch rivals in front of their own fans at Old Trafford. They say good things come to those who wait and let's be honest, we've waited. We waited for a quarter of a century. Yes there was the 4-1 under Rafa, which was amazing but it was still classed as a freak, one-off result, as the Mancs regained composure and strolled to yet another title. Then there was the Danny Murphy years when the underrated midfielder wrote his name in Mersey folklore by scoring a few crucial winners here but let's face facts, these little pockets of comfort have been very few and far between. I hate coming here because it's the same every year, like an Evertonian coming to Anfield. I'm almost programmed to accept the inevitable annual defeat. Everything that could possibly go wrong in football usually does when we play at this ground. Referees buckle under the pressure, players panic, goalkeepers are indecisive. It's as if the Gods conspire against us every time we walk out at Old Trafford and it is our destiny to accept, no matter how we play, we will always come off second best.

But ladies and gentlemen, brothers and sisters, I have important news for you. I think the party's over. I never thought I would hear myself say it but I believe the empire might be crumbling. When their despot dictator abdicated his seat of power in the summer, most observers thought that the transition would be seamless. A case of the keys to the castle being handed from one Glaswegian to another with the simple message of continuity. Only problem was the man chosen to replace the evil dictator was none other than the hapless David Moyes. Now where have we heard that name before? Didn't he used to manage the club of clichés, you know, the smaller club on Merseyside? Yes, that's the bloke. The one who failed to win a single match at Anfield in over a decade in charge, and coined the laughable phrase 'Everton, the people's club'. Yes, I'm afraid that's him. What young David didn't realise though, when he was handed the poisoned chalice of managing one of the biggest clubs in world football, is that his influence would not extend beyond the club. So unlike his predecessor he would have no control over the media, the Premier League, the FA and most of all, the referees. Ferguson was the master of his domain. He had the journalists eating out of his hand. The League danced to any tune he played and the referees were terrified to give a decision against them. It was no coincidence that whenever Liverpool were due to play United there would always be a derogatory newspaper article in the run-up to the match, usually regarding a Liverpool player wanting to leave or some other fictitious nonsense. And it was Ferguson's fingerprints that were always on the trigger. Which other club could just pull out of the FA Cup and have a lucrative mid-season break in Brazil and come back refreshed? The rest of us aren't allowed to. As their fans song says 'we're Man United and we do what we want'. Well not anymore you don't. The press have been ungagged. The referees and linesmen have been giving decisions against them and the playing field for the first time in years is level. And d'you know what, the fuckers don't like it.

Our day starts in Ally's pub at ten bells. After a couple of liveners, about ten of us get the train across the thirty five miles of no man's land and into Manchester's Oxford Road. There's quite a few match heads on it and the police are in no mood to let us out of the station into the city centre. So we are persuaded to get the train, the one stop, straight to the ground. It's no big deal as we'd have only had time for one or two anyway. The short walk under the Munich tunnel past the suits and tourists is uneventful. Now we've got an hour to kill outside our end to basically stand around poking fun at some of the most ridiculous looking fans in the league. Most of them look like they're about to start off on a charity fun run with stupid hats and fancy dress on. Me and Smig have our photo taken with the four obligatory leprechauns. What is it with leprechauns at Old Trafford? We must play them here around Paddy's day ever year, hence the need for knobheads to dress up in all this cheap Irish paraphernalia. They're not even decent leprechauns. I mean if they had a proper long ginger beard instead of that synthetic thing and a bit of decent gear on, WOAH. Hang on, hang on, I can't believe I'm actually discussing the merits of what makes an acceptable leprechaun. Just wait there a mo while I put my head down the toilet again and flush. Ah that's better, anyway, now where was I?

The coaches are arriving and all the usual faces are streaming past us. Everyone from Roy Bentham to Bernie Allen to Mark Blears, Dava Hardman, the legendary Lenny Woods and a cast of thousands, all veterans of this familiar scenario. The Halewood lads, Jeff, Mono and Keith are always well turned out. They stroll by looking more like an Edwardian shooting party in their tweed jackets and brogues. A lot of Scousers over the years have gone in for that role reversal thing, where the lads from the city dress like country squires and the hicks from

Me and Smigger humouring some Man United leprechauns.
We're the ones without the hats.

the sticks wear garish slogan gear with baseball hats on the wrong way
and twenty earrings, which they imagine everyone in the city is
wearing. It's a mixed up, muddled up, shook up world, except for Lola,
as The Kinks once said.

We're in the ground and I'm next to lucky Luke and there's a
positive feeling all around. The Mancs are giving us the usual barrage
of abuse of 'murderers, murderers, murderers' but they are soon
silenced when we start to absolutely dominate for the complete ninety
minutes. It's a weird feeling coming here and being in total control for
the whole match, as it's not something I'm used to. Even the non-
believers, the rival managers and some of the anti-Liverpool brigade
in the media are now describing us as title challengers. No wonder I

can't sleep at night. I'm awake at four in the morning thinking 'imagine if we actually won it, how mad would that be'. I could be stuck at the traffic lights and my mind will slowly wander and I'll think 'no, surely not, we couldn't'. And then I think 'what happens if we do?' I might just have a heart attack and die of happiness.

We should have had a penalty in the first five minutes when old microphone head Fellaini had a couple of digs at Suarez when he was in the box. The ref finally gave us a spot kick when Rafael handballed in the area on 34 minutes. He could've gone for it, as he had already had a yellow but Clattenburg, the ref, showed leniency. Gerrard smashes the ball into the net and the crowd go wild. Some fat bloke decides he needs to kiss someone and I am the unlucky recipient. A full on smacker right in the middle of me forehead. You would've thought he would have at least made some idle conversation beforehand but no, straight for the bear hug and kiss. Good job the sniggering Kirkby Three from the club in Soho after the Fulham game aren't anywhere near. They would've seen that as irrefutable evidence of gay-ness, and demanded a kangaroo court retrial. Phew, close shave. I make a mental note to change places after half time. It's been a dominant first half and we head down to try and get a beer and find somewhere to smoke. By the time I've sorted myself out and had a gab to Vinny, Geoffo and Liam, we score the second. I didn't even know the game had restarted. I've just got to the top of the stairs when the places explodes. There's people on the floor, there's people on their seats, it's utter chaos. We know this is it. The Mancs are on the rack. This is our moment. I finally reach Luke. "What happened?" "Gerard, another penalty" he says, but I can't even hear myself think. Our end is going doolally. They sense it. Then a third penalty but this time Stevie hits the post. Imagine scoring a hat-trick of pennos at Old

Trafford. I think they once went about eight years without getting one awarded against them, let alone getting one scored against them. That's when the refs weren't allowed to give crucial decisions against Fergie's boys. Well those days seem to be over. There's yet another one that could've been given after Sturridge has his legs taken from under him. But I think three pens out of five appeals at Old Trafford is quite sufficient.

Luis Suarez doesn't like being left out so he calmly dispatched the third on 84 minutes. But in all reality we could've had six or seven on another day, but I'll happily take the 3-0. Vidic got sent off for the fourth time against us, maybe even a little harshly but hey, who gives a toss. We've had a million and one decisions against us here so there'll be no tears shed in our house tonight. This is utter humiliation for the hosts as their fly-by-night fans head for the exits long before the final whistle. At the end the team and manager walk across the pitch to applaud the mass ranks of Redmen. It's moments like this that as a football fan you saviour for a lifetime. This is why we are here. This is why we do it. That's why I said at the beginning of this piece that there are very few things in life that are more pleasurable than this. And at this present euphoric moment in time I cannot think of anything more satisfying.

The happy hordes are preparing for their annual half an hour lock in when shock of all shocks, the stewards open the gates and release both sets of fans at the same time. This is unusual. This hasn't happened for years. It's all a bit chaotic as you've got delirious Scousers bouncing in the streets mixed in with some extremely unhappy Mancs. Inevitably there's little scuffles breaking out here, there and everywhere, but nothing major. It's more a case of both sets of fans verbally abusing each other, with the odd sneaky dig being landed through the crowds.

I've seen far worse here over the years though. After some games it used to be like World War Three outside, but the Greater Manchester Police have got it well sewn up nowadays. The crowds filter away as we wait for the train to Oxford Road. We pass the time by taking the piss out of United's vast contingent of foreign support. Those day trippers and tourists with those horrendous half-half scarfs, you know the ones with both teams names on. Half Liverpool Half Man U, absolute sacrilege against everything that supporters hold dear. The biggest rivalry in English football and there's both names on the idiots scarf. To wear one should be made a hanging offence. I thought wearing jesters hats was bad enough but this is a new low in the sanitisation of modern football. How did we allow our game to sink to this murky commercial level? In this X Factor age of reality shows and dumbing down the half-half scarf is the ultimate symbol of tasteless merchandise shite. Hopefully this is as low as we can go and all fans will reject this nonsense. But don't hold your breath because modern football is geared to sell its soul to any mug who will buy into it.

We finally get the train to Oxford Road and it seems to be mainly Liverpool on it, so there's no unwanted surprises. As soon as we get off there's an announcement saying the Liverpool train is leaving in two minutes over the bridge, so there's a bit of a stampede. And before you can say 'David Moyes is a football genius' we are on our way back home to the Promised Land. About twenty of us pile off the train and even the guards at the station are hugging us and shaking hands as if we've just come back from the front line. Lime Street echoes to the sound of "We are Liverpool" as we troop off to the Picture House to be greeted by a mass of pissed happy Reds who are about six or seven pints ahead of us. This is what I love, the whole camaraderie of it all.

Besides Ally, there's Tony Gill, Bobby, Tommy Sutton, Fat Eddie and even me old mate John Heron. It's party time folks. We hit Ma Edgies and sing a few Kop classics. Then we squeeze into the Yankee Bar which as usual is manic. Next stop is down to the Victoria Cross (Neds) where we see Patto, Tommy Trouble and Dicko and sing some more. Bucko's trying to get us to go up to Slater Street to meet Ricky Lambert of Southampton, who's with young Michael, but I'm going nowhere. I'm sure Mr Lambert is a nice chap but he could be with Lionel Messi and Pele for all I care. We've just beaten the Mancs 3-0 and all I want to do is sing footy songs, without bouncers telling me to calm down. I have no idea how I got home. It could've been by spaceship for all I know. I have vague memories of watching Match of the Day but just in case I missed anything the first ten times, I decide to watch it again every night the following week. Oh Brendan Brendan Brendan, when you were given the job of leading the troops into combat, I stood alone. The doubters doubted. I was shouted down when I spoke out against them. I for one had faith. Now they have all seen the light. Let's make this our season. Let us seize the moment and make history together. And then, and only then, can we live happily ever after.

Saturday 22nd March 2014 – 3pm kick-off
The first and only 3pm away kick-off

Cardiff 3 Liverpool 6

It just keeps getting better. No matter what happens between now and the end of the season, this has still been the best campaign for 25 years. Every week it seems to be goals, passion and excitement and the fans are absolutely buzzing off it. Smigger is sitting this one out courtesy of a one-match ban imposed by his missus. Something about responsibilities and a family party, etc. I would've put an appeal in and tried to get the ban overturned, but then I've always been a selfish bastard when it comes to footy. He's gutted he's not travelling because any Red who's spent years following his team through the barren times wants to be there when it finally clicks. We promise to keep in phone contact every couple of hours to keep him up to date.

It's a strange understated start to the day. I meet Ally on the windswept empty station of Bidston, just south of Birkenvegas. It's about 8.30am and we're here to get the little two carriage train to Wrexham. It feels a bit weird. There's only two of us, a couple of cyclists and a stray goth. It all seems a far cry from your usual start, at a cavernous Lime Street with all kinds of shady characters giving you the 'half a nod'. Not the full recognition of a full nod and conversation, just the 'half a nod' and maybe an 'alright' if you're lucky. Nobody wants to look too keen to be mates, unless they're pissed of course. Matchday etiquette has always been, keep it cool on the outward journey and go mental on the way back. Don't ask me why, it's just always been that way.

We get to Wrexham and after a short wait we get the Birmingham train and dive off at Shrewsbury. From here it's just over two hours through small rural stations like Church Stretton, Craven Arms, Ludlow and Abergavenny. There was even one place called Gob Owen and let's be honest, I think the majority of us would like to have gobbed Owen when he signed on the dotted line for that hateful team from Manchester. With perfect timing the last drops of our carry-out are swigged as the train pulls into Cardiff Central. We're supposed to be meeting all the lads in the Great Western by the station but when we get there it's all Cardiff fans. A quick phone call to Captain Bucko reveals that they're round the corner in Bunker bar. Danny Giles phones from home to see what's happening. As I've said before Danny loves a bit of scaremongering. This time he's telling me that the Great Western is where all the Evertonians got attacked. It's as if he's almost willing the same to happen to us. We meet Bucko and them and watch Chelsea demolish Arsenal 6-0. Ritchie and Mercer are in there as is big Ian Mac, young Lee and Tony Casey who's a veteran Road Ender. There's a few Cardiff lads in there but it's fairly mellow. We move onto a little Irish boozer, called Kitty something or other, just along from the Kiwi bar which is supposed to be home to the local hoolie firm. Probably not a great idea to be drinking so close to potential problems, but we have a laugh and begin to walk up to the ground.

As we approach the big crossroads by the stadium, there's about six police cars with flashing lights heading back towards town. "Must've gone off" Ally says. He was right. When we get in the ground I bump into Steve Metcalf who's usually dead laid back, but today he's wide-eyed and animated. The coach we normally travel on, if we're not going by train or car, has been attacked on its way to the ground. It sounds pretty full on. Apparently, the coach emptied of its passengers and an almighty kick off took place in the street. Then another coach from the same company around the corner saw its fellow Kopites in distress and they all piled off. Sounds dead exciting. There's nothing like a bit of mindless football violence to get the old adrenaline going. As much as we all pretend that it's a disgraceful way to behave and a blight on our national game, deep down the first thing you want to know is 'did we hold our own?', 'who got the better of who?'. These things are important.

You can't on one hand be seen as this great fanatical partisan support one minute, and the next be seen as some spineless bunch of nervous wrecks who can't stand up for themselves. And anyway, you don't want to see your fellow Liverpudlians taking a kicking off anyone, so if push comes to shove, of course you want to see your comrades come out on top if there's an unavoidable coming together of the warring factions. It's only human nature. We get into the seats and the sun is shining full on into our faces. I'm in the middle of Luke and Ally with John Buchanan, Danny Nico and all of their excitable Boss Mag gang to our left, enjoying the day out. Then right out of the blue the Bluebirds, who now play in red, have the temerity to score against us. Jordan Much pounced on some sloppy defending to put the home side ahead. Suarez equalised on 16 minutes after a well worked move involving Hendo and Johnson, which really should've set us on our way. But against all odds the cheeky little South Walians scored again through Fraser Campbell. It had been a strange first half and Skrtel nicked one back just before the break to give the game parity. Cardiff, along with West Brom and Stoke, are the only three clubs in the Premier League who open the gates to let you go outside for a smoke. It makes sense instead of choking all the non-believers in the toilets, at the half-time piss fest. Common sense wins the day. All the talk downstairs is of the argy-bargy before the game. It's amazing, like I said before, how everyone seems to buzz off a bit of trouble when we all know that it's naughty and should be frowned upon. Try telling that to the troops. You can see people twenty yards away re-enacting their part in the pre-match shenanigans. Like speeded up tai-chi they describe their role in a kind of hooligan mime show.

Back upstairs the match restarts and the Reds begin to take control. Skrtel scores his second with a header, direct from a corner and King Luis nets after a cheeky back heel from Sturridge. The two-goal cushion gives the crowd a chance to relax, and belt out a few old classics. But we haven't finished yet. Sturridge finally gets on the score sheet after Suarez sets him up after an amazing run to get into the box, just at the right moment. Cardiff pull one back with a simple header which reminds us that although we are irresistible going forward, we are still wobbly as fuck at the back. Then right on the ninety minutes Suarez runs the length of the field and puts pressure on the defender. He then teases David Marshall in goal with a series of dummies, then pokes it home for number six. Another hat-trick for the man they couldn't hang, which puts him on 28 goals in just 25 games. An unbelievable record when you consider that none of those are penalties. That's six wins on the bounce for us now and we really do mean business. We're more or less guaranteed a top four spot, now it's time to really reach out for the holy grail. There's eight games left and we've already broken our Premier League scoring record. The highest previous was 77 goals, we've already notched 82. Where are all those divs who were against Rodgers when he took over now? I hope they've retired from ringing radio phone-ins every other week. It's been like a breath of fresh air this season and hopefully this is just the beginning. We stay to applaud the teams off the pitch and then head out of the ground past the coaches. Just as we're trying to negotiate our way around the perimeter, it goes off again. There's an angry group of Cardiff fans who are far too old to really be involved in a tear-up at their age, but they are. It's roughly even sides. About fifteen young Scousers, late teens to mid twenties, trading blows with blokes who are old enough to be their dads. It's proper toe to toe full-on fisticuffs with no police for ages. There's the weird sight of photographers running through in the middle of it with cameras above their heads like you'd see outside a high profile court case. When the old bill arrive there's a couple of arrests on both sides but as usual, probably not the main protagonists. I have to say though (and I know I'm leaving myself open to criticism here from the great, the good and the high and mighty) I thought the young Reds gave a very good account of themselves. The Cardiff fans were obviously the aggressors but the young Redmen remained on the front foot and never took a backwards step. It looks like us old-timers have left the club in good hands if you know what I mean.

After the ding-dong outside the ground it makes the long walk back into town a little more edgy. Not that anyone is interested in me and Ally but you never know. That main Cardiff nutter involved in the skirmish may well have been some sort of a weightlifter but he was still older than both Brendan Rodgers and Ole Gunnar Solskjaer, so as I say, you never know. As we get to the city centre everyone we phone seems to be getting the early trains out but we fancy a couple of scoops before the long haul journey home. We look into a few pubs but they just seem to be full of local lads and after what's happened today we decide to err on the side of caution. We find a decent place not far from the station where Mi and George are having a couple. Mi lives in London and George in Bournemouth but they were both born and raised in the Pool of Life. We end up in quite a posh gaff called the Barocco which is inhabited by a non-football crowd of bohemian arty types and the usual gaggle of middle-aged women who shout 'Oh my God' every other sentence.

The train leaves in ten minutes so we leg it through the town centre like a couple of wheezing geriatrics. We can hear the strains of 'We are Liverpool' in the distance so we know exactly which platform it is without even looking. The train is chocca with all kinds of weird and wonderful people going back to the Valleys after a day out in civilisation. There's a load of Liverpool supporting wools in the next carriage who keep the same three or four songs going for the next hour or so. I might be a happy Red but they've done my head in within fifteen minutes. Good job they're in the next carriage or I might have had to say something. Where's Luke when you need him? You could stick him in there and he would educate the poor souls with a repertoire of ballads and battle songs that would bring a tear to a private eye with a glass eye on the London eye. After a couple of stops we manage to get some seats as the train empties slightly, but we have a problem. With us leaving it until the last minute to dash across town to the station, we have no beer. Luckily our two new mates from the notorious Urchins come to our assistance. Tommy and little Danny save the day by giving us cans of Carling to soothe our aching bones. They're typical Scousers, cheeky, funny, generous and yet as hard faced as they come. The classic mix.

Just after Hereford I had one of those incidents that keeps happening to me on my travels. It was time to go for a wee, so I sidled my way along the carriage up to those Dr Who style curved toilet doors that they have nowadays with all brightly coloured buttons. Ah, you're ahead of me already. Let me finish your honour. I can explain everything. It was all going so well. I pressed to enter, then I pressed closed, took penis out of jeans and proceeded to piss nonchalantly into the bowl. Imagine my surprise when the door slid open and a child of about ten was standing there in shock. I'm mid piss and still holding cock whilst shouting "Hey what are you doing?" The kid makes a run for it but even worse, there's a teenage girl sitting on a flip up disabled seat staring straight at me. She turns away and puts her hand over the side of her face in a mixture of shock and disgust. I'm trying to shake, close the door and put away the offending item as fast as possible. On the way out I apologise to the girl but in all honesty, between me and you, I thought she delayed the 'turning away in shock' thing by a good two or three seconds, if you get me. Fuck knows where the kid went. I got back to my seat and only touched on the subject saying "Blimey, those doors in the toilets are a bit dodgy. It's like Stars in their Eyes. Tonight Matthew I'm going to expose myself."

When I settled down I closed my eyes and imagined what the papers would say the following day 'Dodd caught with pants down again', 'Washed up wordsmith left speechless', 'This man is a danger to society'. I had visions of ex-girlfriends queuing up to sell their stories to the tabloids about how awful I was. "Jegsy wake up. It's our stop." Where am I? Oh yeah, we get off here for the Liverpool train. I must've dozed off.

After changing at Crewe we finally roll onto Lime Street. Dave and Pooley are in town and want to meet us for a quick last pint. To be honest, I'm weighed in but as usual I get talked into it. We meet them in Ma Edgies which is packed with theatre goers. Young Tommy and Danny take one look and realise this is not their scene and head off to the Yankee Bar for a bit of jiggery pokery. I only stay for the one and gratefully accept a lift home off the Dark Mysterious One. It's been another corker of a day. In fact I'm getting quite used to it now. I know it won't last of course, there are bound to be days when things go horribly wrong. But for the moment, I'm how you say in English 'buzzing my tits off'.

Sunday 6th April 2014 – 4pm kick-off

West Ham 1 Liverpool 2

Six games to go and I'm all of a doo-dah. Three aways, West Ham, Norwich and Palace. Three homes, City, Chelsea and finally Newcastle. If we win every one it's ours. Who would've thought that at the beginning of the season? Certainly not the bookies who were giving 33-1 and 28-1. I remember the Dortmund manager, before the season started, saying that the English league is so dominated by the monied clubs of London and Manchester, that the great traditional teams, like Liverpool, will never again be able to win it. Well, here we are with just over a month to go and guess who's top? Yes, I can't believe it either.

Today is another long trek and yet another London away game for us disciples. West Ham is not a team that I dislike, which is rare. Usually I look at the opposition with a degree of contempt but subconsciously I think I've always had a soft spot for the Hammers. Their fans have always been alright and they usually try to play good football. Obviously that's going to go out of the window now that Sam Allardyce is overseeing things. Old 'bison head' has never been one to embrace the creative side of the game, so this will probably be like a trip to Stoke in the days of Tony Pulis. You've just got to try your best to overcome it. Basically get in, get the job done and get back home with the three points. It's a 4pm kick-off but we're still up bright and early to get the 8.38am train. You might think that is far too early but there is a method to our madness. It was the Grand National yesterday and once the hangovers have cleared, the southern softies will want to get back to the leafy lanes of suburbia. And anyway it gives us time for a decent gargle before the game starts. The train is surprisingly empty so we make camp in first class and enjoy a few of the benefits. The Captain greets us as usual as we arrive in Londinium. My mate Zug who lives in Reading is also there, waiting to be led astray. First bevvy of the day is quaffed in The Euston Rocket on the main road. There's quite a few Reds in there but no-one you know properly. Just the usual "alright mate" etc. So we get the tube from St Pancras to Liverpool Street where we get off and have a few liveners in The White Hart. The weather's alright so we just sit outside and watch the world go by. It really is unique, old London town, one of the great melting pots of the world. Every colour, creed, race and religion all thrown together in one big clash of cultures. Nothing

Team photo en route to Upton Park

shocks you down here. All rules of fashion have been well and truly ripped up and tossed in the bin. If a bloke walked past you with a termite mound on his head no-one would bat an eyelid. Your mate would just say "there's a bloke with a termite mound on his head" and you'd just go "I know, yeah". Whereas in Liverpool you'd get three months in jail for just wearing the wrong brand of training shoes. To say it's a different world is the mother of all understatements.

We move on to a pub by the station called funnily enough The Railway, and it's absolutely full of Redmen. The Everton v Arsenal game is on and the bluenoses batter the gooners 3-0 which looks like we are going to get a minimum Top 3 place now. The Liverpool fans are in good voice, entertaining the locals with their vast repertoire of songs, wit and wisdom. Smigger has to get up to the ground early as he hasn't got a ticket. I have complete faith in him to somehow gain entry because he is one of the original blaggers. He was ducking and diving around football grounds when most of today's attendance were doing wheelies on their BMX's wearing Batman masks. Needless to say he got sorted and presented himself fit and ready for duty before kick-off. We still had to get from Liverpool Street to Upton Park and the clock was ticking. We have a few communal photos on the platform with some fellow Reds who we'd just bumped into. We finally get off at Upton Park station and leg it to the ground.

It's only a couple of hundred yards but back in the 70's and 80's it was probably the scariest walk to a ground in the league, or maybe Middlesbrough just edged them off top spot but it was still bad. Scousers had their own unique fashion in those days and although everyone eventually copied us, for a good few years we stood out like aliens and Upton Park was always a big test for us. Thankfully now you can get to and from a ground without having to feel as if you are part of some crazy action movie. One minute you'd be bouncing around like a low grade, poor man's Jackie Chan, the next minute you're trying to be anonymous by trying to mingle in with the cockney geezers in your claret and blue Fred Perry. Kids these days, they don't know they're bloody born. Thirty years ago if you got back to Lime Street from West Ham with your heart still beating, and still in possession of two arms, two legs and a head, the day was classed as a success. Nowadays if somebody called you 'a big puff' they would probably be given life imprisonment and there'd be a three hour documentary on the awfulness of today's football fans. Where did it all go wrong? Anyway, we amble along to the ground mixing with rival fans and everyone's well behaved, and yes, it does feel weird for an old spunker like me. I know I've been a bit mischievous before, taking the piss out of the new found niceties of football but it does genuinely feel strange to not be the target of some sort of animosity. Maybe that's why so many people got so over excited about the argy bargy at Cardiff the other week. Maybe it's that base testosterone-fuelled need for some sort of tribal confrontation that groups of men have always had since time began. It doesn't matter if you're on a south sea island, the jungles of central Africa or downtown LA, large groups of blokes have always buzzed off having a bit of a ruck with their bitter rivals. You can fill as many TV studios as you want with psychologists and academics pontificating about broken families and role models etc, but the bottom line is, we are all animals. And like all animals, the human being is no different. When authority isn't watching, or on its guard, people misbehave in an unbelievable way to each other. You only need to look at the people we put our trust in, police, politicians and priests. As soon as you turn your back they're pulling stunts that even prisoners on death row would find shocking. So what hope is there for us lot?

I am quite fond of a rant but even I don't know how I got to this stage. I've obviously gone off on a bit of a tangent about mindless violence and forgot that I've got to get into the ground quickly to cheer the mighty Reds on. I'll have to make a mental note not to lose sight of what I'm supposed to be going on about. It's like being in the 4x100m relay team and someone passing me the baton and I just fuck off over the seats and out of the stadium and down the road. I must remain focused on the task ahead, which is to bring you the story of our away day match experience, and not get too distracted (slim chance of that methinks).

As predicted the game is a tough old battle. Mr Bison Head has obviously ordered his players to just launch long balls into the box in the hope that Andy Carroll gets on the end of one. It's a difficult thing to defend but Skrtel and Sakho who came in for the injured Agger did really well. The breakthrough came two minutes before half time when Gerrard set Suarez free and Tomkins handballed it for the Hammers. As cool as you like Stevie sends the goalie the wrong way and everything seems to be going to plan. That is until right on the whistle when Carroll puts his hand in Mignolet's face just as he's catching a high ball. The ball falls loose to Guy Demel who pokes it into the net. The linesman flags but unbelievably the ref overrules him after a lengthy debate. It's a shocking blunder by the ref but we just have to get in there at half time and regroup. Brendan took Coutinho off and replaced him with Lucas Leiva which might be seen by some as a bit negative but in reality it worked a treat. West Ham had one more chance when Carroll hit the bar with a header, but the Reds completely controlled the second half. Suarez hit the cross bar twice with two great efforts and Stevie wrapped up the points with his second penalty after Flanno was upended in the box. It was a debatable one but, after referee Taylor's first half fuck up, it was only us getting what we deserved. The final whistle is greeted with cheers of relief as yet another game is ticked off in this amazing season.

Five to go, starting with City at home next week, which should be a real humdinger. Every match now, the tickets are like gold, especially the away games. It's gonna go to the wire and my nerves are all over the place. I leave the ground and head to the station on my own. I get a call off Smigger who's behind me somewhere saying his dad has been rushed into hozzy so he really needs to be on the 7pm back from Euston. He's cutting it fine as it's gone six now, and we've got to get across more than half of London and change tubes. I bump into Keith from Halewood and sit with him on the train. It's a race against time as me and Smig are on the same train ticket. I think I'm supposed to be his carer, which is not a million miles from the truth. Basically our ticket says that one can't travel without the other, so I wait by the platform after getting a few cans. He arrives a-huffin' and a-puffin', with four minutes spare. Bucko has managed to cajole Ritchie and Merce to miss it and have another hour with him in the capital. I have no such option. We get collared in first class so we have to pay a £15 upgrade to the clicky. It's supposed to be £15 each but we strike a deal with the conscientious little tyrant. Something along the lines of buy one get one free. Smigger's not drinking. He's got other things on his mind. He doesn't want to be going to the hospital stinking of ale, so I drink his share. We get off in Liverpool and he disappears into the night. He needs to be sensible and attend to family matters with a cool rational head. Me, on the other hand, I don't need to be any of the above, so I bump into Tony Casey and head off to Ally's pub to toast the Redmen. I'm still there when the double act that is Ritchie and Mercer roll into town, an hour later. It's been another major step on the road to the Promised Land. Just five more games from a glory that, if it happens, would rate even more spectacular than the miracle that was Istanbul. I am genuinely pissing my pants with excitement.

Sunday 20th April 2014 – 12pm kick-off

Norwich 2 Liverpool 3

It's been a crazy week since I last spoke to you. First of all, we had the amazing 3-2 win over Man City at Anfield on the Sunday, where it seemed that the whole city centre rocked deep into the night. A truly fantastic game of football with huge significance in the race for the championship. And when the hangovers had cleared we smartened ourselves up and gathered again at the famous old ground on Tuesday to pay our respects to the 96 on their 25th anniversary. As usual it was an emotional day with heartfelt speeches from both the managers of Liverpool and our dear rivals Everton. One day justice will be achieved but as I've learnt in the past, these things take time. Too much time.

Back on the pitch, City dropped two points at home to bottom club Sunderland in midweek and even the bluenoses got done at home by Palace 3-2, which gave me the double pleasure of seeing Everton get beat and picking up a tidy sum off Ladbrokes. So all in all, not a bad week in the house of Dodd. Our next stop in this mad old season full of surprises is Carrow Road, home of Norwich City on Easter Sunday. With the kick-off time at a mind boggling, eye watering midday, 12pm. That's right folks, the furthest ground in the Premier and the hardest drive and the kick-off is brought forward to the earliest start of the season. Common sense is still in very short supply amongst the incompetents who run our national game. Barclays, the sponsors of the Premier League have this season been running a marketing charm offensive which in a nutshell says football is all about us, the fans. There have been cheesy adverts on TV and slogans on billboards around grounds patronising the faithful. The league itself use that cringe-inducing phrase 'football family' when in reality it's complete and utter bollocks. Sky Sports TV call the shots and to make us feel like they care, some gel headed suit, probably a Chelsea or Arsenal fan, in some advertising agency thinks of a new buzz word or slogan to keep the natives happy. Well it's all crap. They make it damn near impossible to attend every match but as usual they underestimate the tenacity and determination of Liverpool's amazing fanbase.

I awake in a state of dizzy confusion at 3.45am banging into walls and putting my jumper on inside out. I prowl around the house trying to make as little noise as possible as I gather my things ready for the off. It seems as if every sound is magnified in the dead of night. Even though I'm creeping around like an intruder, each step creaks as if I'm in the Hammer House of Horror. I open the kitchen door and it sounds like something off the Adams family. I only want a quick cup of tea before I go but when I put the kettle on it sounds as if I'm launching NASA's latest space station. I abort the mission and just head out to the car and hit the road.

With the streets being quiet I make it to Kirkby in 25 minutes, where I watch and wait as the silhouette in house number 14 gets busy. Finally the door opens and he makes his appearance under the cover of darkness. Apparently I'm early but in reality I'm not, I'm spot on. I check yesterday's text. Yep, it says 'be at yours between 4.30 and 5am'. It's officially 4.40am and by my reckoning that is between half four and five every day of the week. The next step is to find Griff's address in the unchartered scrubland that is Rainhill. We arrive the same time as

Pooley and put our gear in his car and park mine up until Monday. The pressure is off me now. I've done my little bit. "Norwich please sir and don't spare the horses." We do well. We're past Kettering before we stop for brekky and the John Shuttleworth CD has already had an airing. Everything is going to plan and we're well ahead of schedule. Dave, who is Griff, booked the two rooms about a month ago but the only problem was, he booked them on the Sunday night and not the Saturday, which meant that we still had to do this mad early morning drive after all. Everyone else had stayed the previous night so, as we're arriving after a four and a half hour drive, they are all just finishing breakfast. But this is where Griff pulled off his master stroke. He secretly cancelled the Premier Inn and got us a great deal at the Holiday Inn right next to the ground. In fact, it's part of the stadium. Happy fuckin' days. Car parked right outside. There's even rooms that look directly onto the pitch if you book in advance. When you check in they give you a list of Do's & Don'ts about them saying stuff like no bevvying in view of the pitch, no team colours to be displayed in your window, only two people in each bedroom while the match is in progress, no banners, no swearing and the list goes on. Now you know as well as I do, if you didn't have tickets and your mate had a room facing the pitch, you know exactly what would happen. It would be like the monkey house at Chester Zoo. There'd be about twenty of you bouncing all over the beds with ale going everywhere, bare arses pressed against the windows. In fact if Norwich stay up that's the plan for next year. You could actually have the list of rules and tick each one off as you break them.

Whaddaya mean I'm an irresponsible, immature fool who gives football fans a bad name? Surely it's written into our contracts that we have to act daft and sing un-politically correct songs at our rivals. If you want to sit in peace and quiet and obey the Thought Police I suggest you go to the theatre and leave the footy to us. The game kicks off and young Raheem Sterling scores an absolute belter after four minutes. He receives the ball about 25 yards from goal and absolutely wallops it into the net. The great start is made even better when Raheem sets up Luis Suarez to sidefoot home yet another goal against Norwich City. How they must hate the sight of King Luis down here in Norfolk. They probably have nightmares of him biting heads off canaries and smiling a sinister toothy grin as he haunts the highways and byways of a terrified East Anglia.

We get to half time at 2-0 and the massed ranks of Redmen are feeling pretty pleased with themselves. There's that great shared excitement that we are all about to experience something amazing in the history of Liverpool Football Club. Hold onto your hats though brothers and sisters as Norwich pull one back through Gary Hooper on 54 minutes. Mignolet, who's been a bit hot and cold this season, makes a hash of a cross and Hooper scores from close range. The home team are having a really good go and come close a few times before Sterling scores his second and our third with a really nice deflection to calm the nerves. I bet that the first time you've ever seen the word deflection, in a football sense, not preceded by the word 'wicked'. This wasn't wicked at all, it was nice. Norwich give it their all and pull a consolation goal back scored by Robert Snodgrass but the Reds hold on for another precious victory. For the first time this season, we are now seen as the bookmakers favourites to actually win it. With that will come the tension, the pressure, the expectation and all the part-timers who'll want tickets for the last three games. All kinds of people who haven't been all season will appear out of the woodwork claiming to be Liverpool's most loyal, fanatical supporters. I'm just going to enjoy the moment for what it is. Another great away win.

Don't take your eye
off the ball

The travelling Kop
in full voice

Get in there!

We meet up back at the hotel bar which you could cartwheel to from the away section and proceed to check in. It's not facing the pitch but it's still a good room with a connecting door to where Pooley and Griff are staying. I gaze longingly at the comfortable looking double bed and desperately want to get in it, but I can't. I mention to Smigger that my bed looks cosy and how easy it would be to have forty winks. Straight away 'Insomniac of the Year' snaps "You're not going to fuckin' sleep now, the Everton v Man U game is starting in a minute. It's on in the bar downstairs." Peer pressure. I always succumb to it. We've commandeered a big round table and it's full of beer and happy Redmen. Some of the Norwich team with their little toiletry bags are standing behind us. I think it's something to do with sponsors or something. Snodgrass is there but I've got to be honest, I don't recognise many of them. They're not a high profile team. I would've done when I was a kid because you had every sticker collection and magazine going. Just then somebody notices their Dutch player, Ricky van Wolfswinkel walk past. Quick as a flash Smigger says "Who needs Ricky van Wolfswinkel when we've got Rip Van fuckin' Winkle. This lazy bastard was thinking of getting his head down before", he tells the vicious circle. Amazingly I get some sympathy. The general consensus is that a kip would be a great idea but the downside, is that everyone is in total agreement, that you'll feel fucked all night because you never wake up properly. Well sorry to break this to you chaps but I can switch off for an hour, wake up and feel rejuvenated, refreshed and ready to rock and roll until the death.

Within minutes I've escaped and am in the lift looking back at my reflection thinking "Jesus! What happened?" How did I go from being a fresh faced Anny Road Boot Boy to looking like Bill Shankly with glasses? Where did the years go? Nothing against Uncle Bill but he was no Brad Pitt if you know what I'm saying. I hit the sack and am awake, showered and back downstairs in one hour and ten minutes. The lads have just left to go back to The Complete Angler so I catch them up in no time. I forgot to say, Bucko is staying over which is a bonus, so no doubt he'll be wanting to bunk in our room later. He can get in with Smigger. I don't think I could handle him snoring down my lughole all night. He's got previous. I remember he bunked in with me and Danny in Oslo a couple of years ago. It sounded like the pair of them were having a log-sawing competition in stereo. I'm glad he's staying though as he's the unofficial Minister of Fun, the spark that lights the flame. Everybody needs a Bucko in their life. Maybe we should think about hiring him out for parties and corporate events. Who knows?

We're doing well. We bump into a few other stray Redmen and serenade the Easter Sunday clientele as we stagger from pub to pub spreading our happiness along the way. Other cities would be less accommodating but Norwich just go along with it. I have no idea if they're just humouring us, grinning and bearing it or actually enjoying our company. The truth is we're probably too delirious to even notice any adverse reaction to our self-assured bravado. We call it a day around midnight and somehow manage to wobble back to the hotel in one piece. We've lost Griff but no doubt he will almost certainly have used the services of Norwich's taxi industry to ferry him home.

Smigger and the Captain are awake before me and are making noises about breakfast. The other two are already down there. It's not an easy bunk. The breakfast room must've been like a blaggers convention yesterday so we've got no chance of a freebie this morning. Initially they want 15 rips off us but we get it down to £10 with some sort of voucher and it's crap. If I was one of those busybodies who posts everything on Trip Advisor, I'd say room nice, brekky dreadful. I mean it's not like we pay for our breakfasts very often, so when we do we expect certain standards to be upheld.

We take Bucko to the station, bid him farewell and then begin the mother of all drives home. I'm certainly glad it's not me who's jockeying for position amongst the Bank Holiday traffic jammers. I just want to get home to my bed. To break up the journey we decide to stop at a Burger King where for no apparent reason we decide that we each have to order our food with a speech impediment. Yes I know it sounds stupid and puerile but you have to alleviate the boredom somehow. So lisps, stutters and weirdly an Elvis impression get us crying with laughter at the counter, much to the bemusement of the poor girl tasked with taking our order. We journey on and finally reach our starting point in Rainhill. We shake hands and congratulate Pooley on another magnificent piece of driving, then me and Smig head off to Kirkby in the Dodd-mobile. I finally arrive home about 6pm with all my hopes and dreams still intact. Three to go; the hateful Chelsea at home, Palace away and then hopefully we lift the trophy at home to the Geordies in the last game. As the slogan says 'Keep calm and carry on' but how can you keep calm when you can almost see the Promised Land ahead of you?

Monday 5th May 2014 – 8pm kick-off

Crystal Palace 3 Liverpool 3

Oh dear, oh dear, oh dear. What can I say? I feel like we've been climbing this mountain together and then all of a sudden, with the summit in sight, we get caught in an avalanche. It's as if I'm hanging on for dear life from a random branch as everything around me cascades downwards to the depths of despair. Maybe it's not a branch I'm clinging to. Maybe the branch is just a metaphor for clutching at straws. And more importantly, maybe I'm writing this too soon after the extraordinary events that took place last night in south London. Perhaps I should've waited a few days before I put pen to paper. But on the other hand, it might be some sort of therapy for me to get this out of the way while it's still raw… very raw.

It all started last weekend against the loathsome organisation that is Chelsea Football Club, with their preposterous, presumptuous, pretentious, pompous prick of a manager trying to kid the media into thinking he'd pulled off another tactical master stroke. It wasn't. Gerrard unfortunately slipped over and they got lucky. Ten men behind the ball and a mistake gifts them and their odious fans a painful win. No stroke of genius that the ego of Mourinho would have you believe. Later that day City beat Palace away to move within three points of us, with a better goal difference and a game in hand. Advantage City. We've just to win our last two and hope that the Mancs slip up in their two remaining ones. The Chelsea defeat hurt. Just the pure manner in which they won was galling enough but after eleven straight wins you have to almost accept that it has to come to an end sometime. Just a pity it was against those bastards.

I'd been looking forward to the Palace game for ages. One last blow-out before I disappear back into normal society for three months to do things that everybody else does; weekends away, meals out, maybe even a spot of mud wrestling with a couple of busty, economic migrants. As I say, just the usual type of normal activities. I turn the phone on about 9am and there's a voicemail from a very concerned sounding Smigger. I ring him straight back and it's bad news. His dad has just passed away this morning. Obviously he has to pull out, which is a blow, but there's more important things to attend to. The train is packed so Dave Kirby and Gary have to sit further up the carriage, while I sit with an empty reserved seat next to me. There's some sort of dance troupe in the carriage which seems to consist of fat kids and loud mothers. Problem is there's not enough seats and they're getting louder and looking at the empty spec beside me. I'm trying to put on my most unwelcoming face to fend off the fatties, when I'm saved by old friend Cathy Long, who is in desperate need of a sit down.

It's beneficial to both of us as she gets a seat and I get someone to rant at for the next two hours. By the end of the journey, she probably wished she'd just stood up the whole way by the toilets, or even climbed out onto the roof of the train as if she was on the Calcutta to Rajasthan Express. The reason for this is that Cathy has a very special employer. She is in the privileged position of working for the … wait for it… the Premier League. Yep, she's kind of a fan's liaison officer, I think. I don't know the exact proper job title but it's to do with how supporters spectate or spectators support and all that kind of stuff. My eyes light up at the thought of being able to ramble onto someone about all my gripes concerning modern football for the entire journey. Here I am, a person who spends most of his life moaning, about basically anything, and I'm sitting next to someone whose job it is to take steps to make sure our game is a more enjoyable experience. Right, where do I start. We discuss everything from ticket allocation, to ticket pricing, kick-off times, policing, the Hillsborough enquiry, racism, the media, irritating political correctness, tokenism, hooliganism, the uniqueness of LFC, mad banners, bad manners and everything else in between. And you know what, I feel cleansed. I feel like there is hope. We need people like her. In fact another ten or twelve would do for a start. People who speak the same language as the rest of us, purveyors of common sense and enemies of bull shit. I hope she progresses up the ladder, because we the nation's supporters need that type of voice. We say goodbye and I meet all the lads on the platform feeling slightly positive and, dare I say, invigorated. All we need now is to dump these bags and get on it.

We check into the Travelodge in Kings Cross and as usual in life, one man's misfortune is another man's good luck, for I, due to Smigger's devastating circumstances back home, now have a big fat hotel room all to myself. A place where I can cough, snore, fart and burp until my heart's content and nobody will know except for me. Sounds like heaven, metaphorically speaking of course. I can't imagine they would allow coughing and boffing in heaven somehow, but you never know. Anyway I'll move on before I get too bogged down into the murky world of bodily functions.

I meet Dave, Gary and Zug downstairs and the four of us head off to London Bridge where we can get off and have a few scoops around Borough market. The area has got a really good vibe to it, with some decent alehouses. We set up camp in the Market Porter where we are joined by Kev Sampson, John Mackin and the brainiest man in the world, Andy Baker. Kev and John know stuff, quite a lot of stuff actually, but Mr Baker knows absolutely tonnes of stuff. Familiar faces pass through the pub; Cliffy Keogh, Rollo, and Paul Leonard pop their heads in. Bucko is doing that really infuriating thing he does. He phones and asks you where you are, then turns up at the nearest pub up the road and wants you lot to go and meet him. Exactly the same thing happened at Norwich. He arrives half an hour after us and knows exactly what pub we are in, but goes to the one over the road and demands we all go over to meet him. Very weird behaviour indeed. For instance, if I was in say Papua New Guinea for three days on my own waiting for him to show, he'd finally arrive and I'd say "OK I'll see you in the Head Shrinkers Arms at 2 o'clock". You can guarantee he would phone at ten past and say "Guess where I am, I'm over the road in the Cannibals Bar and Grill. Come over, it's sound." I mean what on earth is all that about. I'm fucked if I know. God knows what a psychologist would make of it. Anyway we decide to leave him to it and head to a fantastic old coach inn called The George which is dripping with history. It says on the wall that Charles Dickens used to pop in here for a lager top but hang on a mo, it also said that in the Friend at Hand in Russell Square, which is miles away. This could mean that old Charlie Dickens might have been a bit of a gargler in his time.

The clock is ticking and we have to get the overland line to Thornton Heath which is a bit of a hike when your bladder is fit to burst. We get off and leg it into the big boozer opposite. Peter Evo welcomes us with a couple of verses of 'We'll be coming down the road' and everything is set for the Redmen to bite back. Nico and Marc have just driven over from Antwerp and will drive straight back after the match. It sounds a bit mad but it's normal to them. They've been doing it for years. There's loads of Liverpool down for this one but there's not enough tickets to go around, so I'm always impressed with the ingenuity of the Scouse brethren. Some of my old mates bounce past looking pleased with themselves. They've just had Chamakh's complimentaries off from the ticket office. There's people bunking in all over the ground which gives the whole match a bit of a buzz. It feels like the Palace is under siege and the stewards are getting twitchy. Funnily enough the Palace fans have been the loudest at Anfield this season. Far more vocal than some of our really big rivals, so as you can imagine the atmosphere is rocking. What happened here though during the 90 minutes of play was mental. Absolutely astonishing. From a dominant position of being 3-0 up and cruising, to the utter defensive chaos of conceding three in the last 11 disastrous minutes.

I've seen some mad games in my time, second half turnarounds and freak goals etc, but this was just unbelievable. It felt as if the whole away section of Selhurst Park had been poisoned and put in a state of suspended animation. People fell onto their seats with their heads in their hands, others would look to their mates for support. There were tears, there was anger, there was frustration. There was a feeling of 'why didn't we just take the win'. We were never going to topple City on goal average. There were people moaning about substitutions and Victor bloody Moses, and this, that and the other. My thoughts were more along the lines of 'what the fuck was all that about', which wouldn't be a bad title for this book, but I doubt if I'd be able to get away with it. We've let it slip through our hands and we know it. City have two games left, both at home against Villa and West Ham and let's be honest, they're not gonna lose them. In fact they can even draw one and still win the title. Your mates will tell you there's gonna be another twist, or City might bottle it, but in my mind, the game City could and should've lost was the one they won at Goodison. The one when those shameless bitter bluenosed conspirators rolled over to have their tummies tickled by Pelligrini's billionaires. I still feel numb as I write this, briefly our game, as if you needed reminding went as follows. Joe Allen scores with a header on 18, Sturridge and Suarez add another couple on 53 and 55 minutes. Game over you might think. The crowd obviously want more and roar them on with shouts of 'attack, attack, attack' which we do. There's chances missed, penalties turned down and then they get the break, with 11 minutes left. Delaney tries a hit and hope which deflects off Johnson and into the net. Within a couple of minutes the weird looking substitute Dwight Gayle makes it 3-2 and then before you know it, he does it again to basically kill us.

We leave the ground as if we are leaving the scene of a crime, feeling utterly shell shocked. We're supposed to be meeting people by Borough Market again but the first train to leave is a direct one to Victoria which saves all the arsing about of stopping everywhere. A quick change and we're at Euston to drown our sorrows in The George, with Red eyewitnesses. Everyone is split up all over London, so me and Gary grab a taxi up to The Lexington pub on Pentonville Road for a late one. It's full of very pissed, pissed off Scousers and let me tell you ladies and gentlemen, that a room full of unhappy Redmen is not a pretty sight. We bail out about 2am and walk back down to Kings Cross and straight to bed.

I awake to the sound of the phone. Mr Kirby and Gary are in the café up the road having brekky and picking the bones out of last night's capitulation. I squint at the mirror with my pistachio shell eyes and then start to read all the texts. They're all over the top knee jerk reaction ones, but what the fuck does anyone expect. It's only human nature to let off a bit of steam, and have a rant after something which you hold so dear goes so horribly wrong.

I meet the lads, have a quick nosebag and head down to the Euston flyer to meet the others. Everyone has got an opinion. Scapegoats are hunted down and roasted on the sacrificial spit of cynicism. I decide to phone Smigger to see how he's coping and it's he who then ends up consoling me. That's how mad football is. Your mate's dad dies and he's offering me words of comfort and wisdom over a match against Crystal fuckin' Palace, which we didn't even lose. The world has officially gone bonkers. This brings light relief to Bucko and Ritchie when I tell them that Smigger says that we should get our chins up and be positive, etc. "What? You phoned Smigger up for motivation the day after his dad passes away. You fuckin' nutter." That's it then. I have to put up with about half an hour of solid piss taking. I get on the train and sit with Dave Griff and Pooley while the others are scattered around in different carriages. Marty Mullen plonks himself down and we have a gab about where it all went wrong. I just want to get home and chill before I force myself to watch the game again, and then finally write all this nonsense. Dave Kirby phones from further down the train and asks if I fancy a bevvy in town before I get off home. My head's battered, so it's a case of thanks but no thanks. I get an Echo from Lime Street which I still haven't plucked up the courage to read. Maybe tomorrow I'll wake up in a more positive frame of mind, and still believe in miracles. Who knows? City might choke and we'll all live happily ever after. Well that's 19 league away games out of 19 completed. Whatever happens, it's been an absolute stormer of a season, but now we must wait. We must wait for the conclusion to this epic journey.

The Dodd Awards and Season Highlights

Best Game

Everton away 3-3. Proper edge of the seat stuff. The match that had everything. I could easily have put the 4-0'er at Anfield but that was too easy. This was emotionally draining.

Best Goal Celebration By The Team

Flanno, third goal at Spurs. The whole team have a mass pile-on in front of the away end. A classic moment in a memorable match at White Hart Lane.

Best Goal Celebration By The Fans

Stevie lashes home a last minute penalty to beat Fulham 3-2 at Craven Cottage. Cue absolute mayhem amongst the travelling supporters.

Best New Fashion

Beards. We haven't seen proper full on beards in fashion since the Victorian explorers set off to discover far off lands like Middlesbrough. There were goatees about twenty years ago but they started getting worn by bouncers and bizzies which killed their credibility overnight.

But yes, a long overdue, welcome back to the big fuck off beard. Mountaineers, Muslim fundamentalists and tramps are all probably walking around town as if they started it all off, "oh yeah, I've had one for years me. I knew they'd come back in". On the other side of town the pogonophobes will be quietly shitting themselves.

Worst New Fashion

The short back and sides haircut which always makes an appearance every generation. This time it overstepped the mark and wandered into Kim Jung Sum territory. If you want to look like a North Korean dictator whilst bouncing down Slater Street be it on your own heard… literally. I imagine that by the time this goes to press most of the uber-quiffs will probably have been tamed and slightly modified. But if you still want to look like your granddad on all those faded army photographs hidden in the loft, that's your choice. Me? I'm still waiting for the Ziggy Stardust revival.

Worst View In An Away End

Goes to the back of the Lower Bullens Road at Goodison Park. It's like being inside a pillar box whilst wearing a burka, suffering from glaucoma, looking through the wrong end of a telescope out into thick fog.

Worst Hangover

A surprisingly large amount of contenders for this award but I think Swansea just edges it, due to the horrendous journey home.

Best Stewards

Norwich or Sunderland.

Worst Stewards

Chelsea…absolute twats.

The Geordie Award For The Divviest Fans

Clear winners for the 40th year in a row, keeping the Man U Irish leprechauns off top spot, yes you've guessed it, it's the Newcastle fans. The mad thing is they think the rest of the country is in awe of them with their shit songs and lack of dress sense. The reality is somewhat different. Whenever we play them up there you can hear fellow Reds saying to each other "Oh no, look at the state of this one". And the reply would be along the lines of "That's fuck all. Look at the kip of these two" and so on and so forth.

The W.T.F Awards

It has to be the eerie, almost ghost like appearance of Alex Ferguson slowly walking behind us on an empty platform in Euston Station on the Thursday after Fulham. An almost dreamlike encounter, like something out of a Hitchcock film. It still haunts me to this day.

Worst Football Merchandise

The half-half scarf. One half Liverpool and the other half whoever you're playing. Just the complete lowest you can go as a football fan. You may as well get one of those strap on accessories that the more adventurous lesbians use and tie it round your head whilst sitting in the Main stand. People will probably respect you a little more.

Worst Ground

Stoke. Isolated in a soul destroying retail park with one shit pub. If there's a queue, get round the back and through the fire door. If stopped, just say I said it was ok.

Best New Song

It's not the best, but it was the song of the season "We are Liverpool, tra la la la la, poetry in motion" and all that.

Worst New Song

"Forza Liverpool Ole". Three words, one Italian, one English, one Spanish. Very clever, very tri-lingual, now fuck off and don't sing it again. It's crap.

Worst Refereeing Decision

Too many. We'll be here all day. Ok, a quick three. Eto's non-sending off in the first minute at Stamford Bridge and then he carries on and scores the winner. Howard Webb, our nemesis, also failed to see Eto hack Suarez down in the area with seven minutes left. Sterling's offside goal at Man City when he was clearly three yards on. What about Mirallas kung-fuing Suarez in the Goodison derby. The list is endless.

The Rush Of Blood To The Head Award

Kolo Toure. Which one would you like Kolo lad? The bizarre oggy at Fulham or the slide rule pass to Anichebe at West Brom? No go on, you choose.

Conclusion

And so it came to pass that the nouveau riche sky blues of Manchester City collected their second Premier League title in three years. Villa and West Ham were comfortably swept aside at the Etihad while we overcame the Geordies at a proud but deflated Anfield. There was no way I could've written this, in the immediate aftermath of the season, as the pain was far too raw to give a measured account. It's only now, after I've come back from a break in Iceland and Orkney, that I can try and make some sense of it all. The gloom has lifted but those faces that filed out of Anfield on that last day said it all. They knew how close we'd been to pulling off what would've been one of the greatest moments in our history. They had dreamed, like I had dreamed but it wasn't to be. We all had to endure the sight of City celebrating their win beaming out of every TV that you looked at. All thinking the same thing "Call that a celebration?" We'd have made that look like Team GB celebrating winning the curling or the archery or something. Or Mrs Sidesaddle from Potburn on the Crimpolene getting the bronze for her orchids at the Southport Flower Show. You just know it would've been madder, bigger and better if we'd have won it. Probably better for English football as well. I don't even know if City use an academy any more. It's just a case of saying "How much do you want?"

But anyway, now that I've had time to think and I've calmed down a little bit, I think it was a great campaign. Heartbreaking yes, but on the whole probably the most exciting one for 25 years. We've got a great young team and a manager that has given us back our belief. Our support is second to none and will always be envied by our rivals. Some will fall by the wayside and be replaced by younger equally fanatical fans who want to share this journey. The die-hards will always be there. Let's just hope that we can build on this momentum and somehow get there in the end. For now though we'll probably all go our own separate ways, renew our season tickets, watch a bit of the World Cup and rest. When August comes around we'll put in some pre-season training at a secret location (THE PUB), where we'll discuss tactics and be ready to do it all over again for the umpteenth time. Another year older and hopefully another step closer to that elusive Premier League title. And if Brendan ever needs any advice, or maybe just a bevvy and a bit of a chat, I'm sure he knows where to find us. Anyway you beautiful Reds, it's been an absolute joy writing this and I hope you've had a laugh reading it. Until next season... Cheers.